THE AUSTRALIAN
Women's Weekly

I want to make food at home that's really good and, simultaneously, good for me, my family (especially my new grand daughter!) and friends — and I bet you do, too. And contrary to popular opinion, food that's healthy doesn't have to be bland or boring, as you'll see by flicking through *Low-fat Food for Life*. Start cooking and you'll be surprised by how easy it is to stick to food that's low in fat but high in flavour – a diet that will benefit every body.

Pamela Clark

Food Director

contents

food for life

LEARN THE BASICS OF WHAT TO EAT AND WHAT TO AVOID AND YOU'LL QUICKLY DISCOVER THAT CHOOSING TO EAT HEALTHY FOOD DOES NOT MEAN CHOOSING TO EAT BLAND FOOD

A diet low in fat (particularly saturated fat) and high in fresh unprocessed food, coupled with a reasonable amount of physical activity, is generally regarded as a straightforward and simple guide to a healthy life. Such a regime will not only help you maintain a proper weight, it can also help keep your cholesterol and blood pressure levels under control and assist in reducing the risk of heart disease and type-2 diabetes.

While genetics and lifestyle play a part in determining a person's weight, the fact remains that too many of us eat badly. Witness the growth in the takeaway and fast food industries, the increase in the percentage of people who can be classed as overweight or obese, and the growing incidence of type-2 diabetes and heart disease. High saturated-fat intakes have been linked not only to both of these diseases but to certain types of cancer as well.

THE OLD DAYS VS THE PRESENT

In the distant past, our ancestors lived on a diet – consisting primarily of grains, cereals, fruits, vegetables, nuts and legumes – that was relatively low in saturated fat and high in foods that promoted activity. Our diet, however, has evolved into one in which saturated fats and overprocessed foods rule; it's a menu tailored to increase both our blood glucose (sugar) and insulin levels to worrying heights. Pressed for time and blessed with science, we rely heavily on foods that are quick to get to the table and don't need a lot of preparation. Worse, some manufactured and many takeaway foods use large quantities of fat to make bland carbohydrates exciting – think of deep-frying for potatoes.

Carbohydrates

In tandem with lowering our saturated fat intakes, we should also concentrate on consuming more carbohydrates. Carbohydrate foods generally make us feel fuller faster than do fats, give us more energy, help stave off hunger pangs and do not easily convert to body fat. But what are they?

Carbohydrates come mostly from plants, ie., cereals and grains, fruits, vegetables and legumes, but dairy products also contain carbs. Recommended dietary guidelines suggest we eat substantial servings of cereals, legumes, rice and pasta, followed by vegetables and fruits. Dairy products should be eaten in moderation then, in diminishing quantities, meat, sugar, butter and the like can be consumed.

The glycaemic index

While a high-carbohydrate diet is better for us than a high-fat diet, certain kinds of carbohydrate foods are better than others. During the 1980s, nutritional research resulted in the creation of the glycaemic index (GI), a ranking of carbohydrates in foods based on their impact on blood glucose (sugar) levels in the body. Originally developed to help people with diabetes, research is showing that the glycaemic index is also a valid tool to assist in weight loss and heart disease prevention.

Rapidly absorbed pure glucose has the highest GI factor of 100. Carbohydrates that break down slowly and release glucose into the blood stream gradually have low GI values (55 or less), while those that are easily digested and absorbed quickly are considered to have high GI values (70 or more).

Medium (or intermediate) GI foods have values between 55 and 70. Low-fat high-GI food doesn't have to be excluded from a healthy diet when coupled with equal amounts of low-GI food – the result is a healthy diet with an intermediate-GI rating. The most important rule to follow is to eat as wide a variety as possible of low saturated-fat, low-to-medium GI foods.

 Look for this symbol (on left) on packaged products in your supermarket. It indicates the product has been GI tested.

Fibre

Dietary fibre is mainly indigestible plant matter that has no nutritional value. Unable to be absorbed, it acts as roughage to help keep the digestive system healthy and filter excess cholesterol from digestive juices – essential in the maintenance of healthy gut bacteria. High-fibre carbohydrates as a rule have lower GI values and help assuage hunger pangs. A diet high in fibre is beneficial for people with type-2 diabetes and nutritionists advise that a healthy diet includes at least 30g of fibre daily. Good fibre sources are wholegrain cereals, brans and breads, and unpeeled, raw fruits and vegetables.

Saturated fat

Eating too much saturated fat is bad for your health – it raises blood cholesterol more than other forms of fat and has far more kilojoules than carbohydrates or protein. High levels of saturated fat in the diet are linked to increased risk of heart and vascular disease, and certain cancers. The reason we consume saturated fat at all is because it is unavoidable in meat, many dairy products and some vegetable oils; its benefits are that it carries fat-soluble vitamins (A, D, E and K), it provides energy and supplies certain essential fatty acids needed to maintain the structure of cell membranes and form hormone-like substances that regulate the body's biochemistry. It is best for healthy adults to reduce daily consumption of saturated fats to less than 8% of total caloric intake. Saturated fats tend to be solid at room temperature and are found mainly in animal products such as butter, cream, chicken skin, fat on meat, cheese, lard and dripping. They are also found in pies and cakes, snack foods, pastries and oils such as palm and coconut.

Sodium

It's a given that we should all eat less salt (sodium); it can lead to increased blood pressure and the accompanying risk of heart disease and stroke. Still, sodium is essential in our diet – the recommended daily intake is 920mg to 2300mg, but this level can be achieved through the salt found naturally in fresh foods and unavoidably in manufactured foods. Try to choose processed foods that are labelled "no added salt" or "salt-reduced", and similarly try to avoid highly salted foods such as potato chips, salted nuts and most takeaway foods. Instead of using salt at the table, flavour your food with cracked pepper, chopped fresh herbs, lemon juice or balsamic vinegar, garlic, chilli and the like. Make your own mustard, tomato sauce, chutney and sweet chilli sauce – without adding salt. Use dried ground spices, onions and leeks, wine and vinegar in cooking instead of salt.

GI TIPS FOR HEALTHY COOKING

Don't cut or chop food too finely. This ensures you will receive the full benefit of the food's fibre content – the smaller the pieces of food, the less fibrous and the higher the GI rating

Don't overprocess food

Don't overcook food

Acidulate food with vinegar or citrus juice

Make use of a wide variety of grains and cereals, and vegetables and legumes – in as natural a state as possible

Most fruit and low- or no-fat milk or yogurt can be added to breakfast cereals to help lower overall GI

Choose seeded or wholegrain breads over soft-textured plain-flour breads

Eat doongara or basmati rice, kumara or sweet potato, or al dente pasta or noodles in preference to ordinary white potatoes and ordinary rice

Add pulses and legumes, such as split peas, beans, lentils and chickpeas, to soups and casseroles

LOWER-GI FOOD

Doongara and basmati rice
Al dente pasta
Buckwheat, burghul, barley and bran
Rolled oats and other rolled grains
Grainy bread, fruit loaves
Pitta, pumpernickel
Carrots, kumara, peas and corn
Chickpeas, kidney and cannellini beans
Soy beans and other soy products
Apples, pears and oranges
Stone fruits (cherries, apricots and plums)
Grapes, raisins and dried apricots
Tomato soup, lentil soup
Low-fat or no-fat milk and yogurt

HIGHER-GI FOOD

Watermelon, dates, lychees
White rice, white bread, white potatoes
Sports drinks
Waffles, pikelets and gluten-free pancakes made from mixes
Pumpkin, broad beans and parsnips
Bagels, rye bread, water biscuits
Jelly beans, lamingtons and Roll-ups
Frozen tofu and tapioca pudding made with milk

Why lower-GI means a better future

In simple terms, consumption of slowly digested carbohydrate foods (low GI) helps keep up energy levels and assists people with diabetes to manage their blood glucose levels which, in turn, aids their wellbeing and reduces the risk of health complications. High-GI foods are best consumed by athletes during periods of competition when rapid energy boosts are needed, or by people with diabetes when experiencing low blood glucose. It is wise to remember that many high-GI foods, such as potatoes, are useful sources of other essential nutrients such as dietary fibre, vitamins and minerals, and can be included in moderation in a healthy balanced diet.

Additionally, research indicates that those who consume a high-GI diet are at an increased risk of developing type-2 diabetes; diets with a low fibre intake and high-GI almost double that risk. Other indications are that high-GI diets can increase the risk of heart disease when, of course, measured in the context of other considerations such as age, sex, body weight and so forth.

Many experts believe that a lifestyle that works for people with diabetes – regular physical activity and a low saturated-fat, high-fibre diet – are good for the rest of us too. And another bonus to a high-carbohydrate lower-GI diet is the resulting reduction in kilojoule intake.

You can use the GI factor as a guide to choosing foods for optimum weight management, high energy and more stable blood glucose levels. A balanced diet can include a wide array of foods, most of which are natural and wholesome. Simple changes to your diet, such as eating wholegrain bread (rather than white bread), more fruits and lots of vegetables, will find you following a lower-GI eating plan without trying!

The recipes in this book show you how to create low-fat dishes that are both healthy and delicious. As they are also low in saturated fats, they may also help assist in reducing blood cholesterol levels or lessen the risk of future illness.

EAT YOUR VEGGIES!

An apple a day may keep the doctor away, but for keeping well and having a sense of wellbeing, turn to vegetables… five servings a day is the recommended amount. Recent studies indicate that phytochemicals (naturally occurring plant chemicals) and antioxidants (elements that stop free radicals from destroying DNA) contained in vegetables can play a part in reducing the possibility of cancer and heart disease.

Eat more tomatoes (a good source of vitamin C), spinach (loaded with B vitamins, iron and folate) and broccoli (rich in fibre and calcium).

Keep washed and trimmed celery, carrot, fennel, cucumber and the like in the refrigerator; you're more likely to snack on them if they're ready to eat. Juice vegetables when they look a little tired.

Serve a green salad with every main meal – keep it simple so it's less of a chore to make. Use fresh lemon juice or balsamic vinegar and finely chopped herbs for a dressing.

Make fresh pasta sauces from vegetables – the Italians have for centuries. Broccoli or cauliflower florets, sugar snap or snow peas, chopped red onion, sliced mushrooms, cherry tomatoes or finely shaved fennel can be tossed into just-drained hot pasta and eaten immediately.

Think about roasting or grilling your vegetables. Carrots, pumpkin, kumara, yams, turnips and beetroot can all be roasted in a hot oven and are perfectly delicious without adding anything to them. And eggplant, capsicum, zucchini and whole red onions are delectable grilled on a hotplate or the barbecue.

Don't forget how good homemade vegetable soup is, or how easy it is to make a veggie stir-fry with lots of chilli, ginger and garlic.

We are blessed with a wide variety of vegetables available in our supermarkets and greengrocers – so work your way through the huge selection. There's nothing wrong with eating the same old standards year in year out, but trying different vegetables can make meals more interesting. Select those in season when at their peak.

	BREAKFAST	LUNCH	DINNER	DESSERT
MONDAY	• Rolled oat porridge (page 12) • 1 apple • 1 slice wholegrain bread	• Cottage cheese and salad on 2 slices of multigrain bread • 1 orange	• Crisp-skinned snapper with stir-fried vegetables and black beans (page 50) • 1 cup cooked brown rice	• Apricot upside-down cakes (page 106)
TUESDAY	• 2 crumpets with unsaturated margarine or Vegemite • 1 small tub low-fat fruit yogurt	• Chilli and lime chicken salad (page 40) • 1 apple • 2 slices wholegrain bread	• Lentil cottage pie (page 57) • Green salad	• Strawberry and rhubarb muffins (page 98)
WEDNESDAY	• Untoasted muesli (page 23) • 1 banana	• 1 cup canned peaches in natural juice • 1 small tub low-fat yogurt (any flavour) • 1 cup orange juice	• Rosemary, brie and sun-dried tomato chicken on corn mash (page 46) • Steamed broccoli and carrots	• Unsweetened small can two fruits • 1 scoop low-fat ice-cream (any flavour)
THURSDAY	• Citrus compote (page 16) • 2 slices toasted multigrain bread with unsaturated margarine	• Kumara and coriander soup (page 28) • 1 wholemeal bread roll	• Herb-crusted lamb racks with kipfler potatoes and leek (page 60) • Steamed brussels sprouts	• Yogurt and mango jelly (page 114)
FRIDAY	• Morning trifles (page 22) • 2 slices toasted wholemeal bread with vegemite or unsaturated margarine	• Rice and chickpea salad (page 38) • 1 pear	• Tofu stir-fry (page 65)	• Chocolate brownie (page 102)
SATURDAY	• Strawberry hotcakes with blueberry sauce (page 26)	• ½ cup baked beans with 2 slices toasted wholegrain bread • 1 apple	• Grilled lean beef steak • 1 jacket potato with small tub low-fat natural yogurt • Green salad • 1 multigrain roll	• Apricot strudel (page 95)
SUNDAY	• Breakfast with the lot (page 20) • 1 small tub low-fat fruit yogurt	• Niçoise salad (page 35) • 1 orange • 1 multigrain roll	• Pork loin with couscous and apples (page 66) • Steamed baby potatoes and green beans	• 2 scoops low-fat ice-cream (any flavour)

breakfasts

corn fritters with roasted tomato chilli jam

PREPARATION TIME 20 MINUTES **COOKING TIME** 1 HOUR 25 MINUTES

You need 2 medium corn cobs, each weighing about 250g after being trimmed.
Roasted tomato chilli jam is best made a day or two ahead to allow the flavours to develop.

1 cup (160g) wholemeal self-raising flour
½ teaspoon bicarbonate of soda
½ teaspoon hot paprika
¾ cup (180ml) no-fat milk
2 eggs, beaten lightly
2 cups (330g) fresh corn kernels
1 small red capsicum (150g), chopped finely
2 green onions, sliced thinly
2 tablespoons finely chopped fresh
　　flat-leaf parsley
ROASTED TOMATO CHILLI JAM
2 medium tomatoes (380g)
1 small red onion (100g), chopped finely
1 clove garlic, crushed
2 teaspoons grated fresh ginger
¼ cup (60ml) lime juice
2 tablespoons brown sugar
2 red thai chillies, chopped finely

1 Sift flour, soda and paprika into medium bowl. Make well in centre of flour mixture, gradually whisk in combined milk and eggs until batter is smooth. Stir corn, capsicum, onion and parsley into batter.

2 Pour ¼ cup batter into heated large lightly greased non-stick frying pan; using spatula, spread batter to shape into a round. Cook about 2 minutes each side or until fritter is lightly browned and cooked through, remove from pan; cover to keep warm. Repeat with remaining batter.
roasted tomato chilli jam Preheat oven to hot. Halve tomatoes; place, cut-side up, on lightly oiled oven tray. Roast, uncovered, in hot oven 30 minutes; chop tomato coarsely. Combine tomato with remaining ingredients in small saucepan, stirring over low heat until sugar dissolves; bring to a boil. Reduce heat; simmer, uncovered, about 40 minutes or until thickened.

serves 4
per serving 5g fat; 1250kJ (299 cal); 1.2g saturated fat; 8.9g fibre; 48.4g carbohydrate; medium GI
tip You can make double the quantity of jam and keep it, covered, in the refrigerator for up to 4 weeks.
serving suggestion Serve with baby spinach leaves.

porridge with rolled grains

We used water to make these porridges, but no-fat milk or various fruit juices are an option, if desired. The amounts given below for each type of porridge are enough to make 4 servings.

GRAIN	Amount	Soaking liquid	Cooking liquid	Cooking time	Makes
ROLLED RICE	¾ cup (75g)	1½ cups (375ml)	¾ cup (180ml)	10 minutes	1¾ cups per serving 0.5g fat; 238kJ (57 cal); 0g saturated fat; 0.6g fibre; 14.8g carbohydrate
ROLLED BARLEY	¾ cup (75g)	1½ cups (375ml)	¾ cup (180ml)	25 minutes	1½ cups per serving 0.1g fat; 276kJ (66 cal); 0.1g saturated fat; 2.1g fibre; 11.5g carbohydrate
ROLLED OATS	¾ cup (60g)	1½ cups (375ml)	½ cup (125ml)	10 minutes	1½ cups per serving 1.3g fat; 233kJ (56 cal); 0.2g saturated fat; 1g fibre; 9.3g carbohydrate
ROLLED RYE	¾ cup (75g)	1½ cups (375ml)	1½ cups (375ml)	50 minutes	1¾ cups per serving 0.5g fat; 248kJ (59 cal); 2.3g fibre; 12.1g carbohydrate
ROLLED TRITICALE	¾ cup (75g)	1½ cups (375ml)	1½ cups (375ml)	45 minutes	1¼ cups per serving 0.5g fat; 244kJ (58 cal); 11.7g carbohydrate

1 Place grain and soaking liquid in medium bowl, cover; stand at room temperature overnight.

2 Place undrained grain in medium saucepan; cook, stirring, until mixture comes to a boil. Add cooking liquid, reduce heat; simmer, uncovered, for required cooking time. Serve warm with toppings of your choice.

toppings

These toppings are enough for a single serving of porridge.

½ cup (125ml) no-fat milk	0.1g fat; 189kJ (45 cal); 0.1g saturated fat; 0g fibre; 6.5g carbohydrate
1 teaspoon honey	0g fat; 94kJ (23 cal); 0g saturated fat; 0g fibre; 22.2g carbohydrate
1 tablespoon low-fat vanilla yogurt	0g fat; 68kJ (16 cal); 0g saturated fat; 0g fibre; 2.4g carbohydrate
pinch cinnamon	0g fat; 6kJ (2 cal)
½ mashed banana	0.1g fat; 240kJ (57 cal); 0g saturated fat; 5.1g fibre; 45.8g carbohydrate
1 tablespoon dried fruit	0.1g fat; 156kJ (37 cal); 0.1g saturated fat; 1.1g fibre; 13g carbohydrate
2 teaspoons toasted shredded coconut	2g fat; 79kJ (19 cal); 1.7g saturated fat; 0.4g fibre; 0.2g carbohydrate

rolled barley

rolled rice

rolled rye

rolled triticale

rolled oats

date and bran muffins

1½ cups (100g)
  unprocessed bran
1½ cups (375ml) no-fat milk
1¼ cups (185g)
  self-raising flour
½ cup (100g) firmly packed
  brown sugar
2 teaspoons ground cinnamon
⅓ cup (90g) low-fat dairy-free
  spread, melted
1 egg
1 cup (160g) finely chopped
  seeded dried dates

1 Preheat oven to moderate.
   Grease 12-hole (⅓ cup/80ml)
   muffin pan.
2 Combine bran and milk in large
   bowl; stand 5 minutes.
3 Stir flour, sugar and cinnamon
   into bran mixture until combined.
   Add remaining ingredients;
   stir but do not overmix. Divide
   muffin mixture among holes
   of prepared pan.
4 Bake in moderate oven about
   25 minutes. Turn muffins onto
   wire rack to cool.

makes 12 muffins
per muffin 4.1g fat; 739kJ
(177cal); 0.8g saturated fat;
5.7g fibre; 30.6g carbohydrate;
high GI

rice porridge with raisins

PREPARATION TIME 10 MINUTES **COOKING TIME** 30 MINUTES

½ cup (100g) doongara rice
½ cup (125ml) water
2 cups (500ml) no-fat milk
1 tablespoon brown sugar
¼ cup (40g) raisins
pinch nutmeg
⅔ cup (160ml) no-fat milk,
    warmed, extra

1   Combine rice and the water in
    small saucepan; bring to a boil.
    Reduce heat; simmer, uncovered,
    until liquid is absorbed.
2   Add milk, sugar and raisins;
    simmer about 20 minutes
    or until rice is tender, stirring
    occasionally. Stir in nutmeg;
    serve warm with extra milk.

serves 4
per serving 0.4g fat; 789kJ
(188 cal); 0.2g saturated fat;
0.7g fibre; 38.6g carbohydrate;
low GI

Doongara rice, also labelled
"Clever Rice", can be found
at your local supermarket

citrus compote

PREPARATION TIME 20 MINUTES (PLUS STANDING TIME)

2 large limes (160g)
3 large oranges (900g)
2 medium pink grapefruit (850g)
2 teaspoons sugar
½ vanilla bean, split
1 tablespoon small fresh mint leaves

1 Grate the rind of 1 lime and 1 orange finely; reserve grated rind. Peel remaining lime, remaining oranges, and grapefruit.
2 Segment all citrus over a large bowl to save juice, removing and discarding membrane from each segment. Add segments to bowl with sugar, vanilla bean and reserved rind; stir gently to combine.
3 Stand, covered, at room temperature 5 minutes; sprinkle with mint leaves.

serves 4
per serving 0.7g fat; 685kJ (164 cal); 0g saturated fat; 6.7g fibre; 33.3g carbohydrate; low GI

Pink or ruby grapefruit have coral-pink flesh and a shell-pink blush to their skin, and are sweeter than the yellow-skinned variety

strawberry smoothie

PREPARATION TIME 10 MINUTES

200g low-fat frozen strawberry yogurt
250g strawberries
1 litre (4 cups) no-fat milk

1 Soften yogurt slightly; cut into pieces. Hull strawberries; cut each in half.
2 Blend or process ingredients, in batches, until smooth.

serves 4

per serving 3.5g fat; 783kJ (187 cal); 2.3g saturated fat; 1.4g fibre; 27g carbohydrate; low GI

mocha smoothie

PREPARATION TIME 5 MINUTES

1 litre (4 cups) no-fat milk
1 cup (250ml) low-fat chocolate mousse
1 cup (250ml) low-fat chocolate ice-cream
1 tablespoon instant coffee powder
½ teaspoon vanilla essence

1 Blend or process ingredients, in batches, until smooth.

serves 4
per serving 4g fat; 896kJ (214 cal); 0.9g saturated fat; 0.2g fibre; 19.3g carbohydrate; low GI

peach smoothie

PREPARATION TIME 10 MINUTES

2 cups (500ml) no-fat soy milk
2 medium bananas (400g), chopped coarsely
4 medium peaches (600g), chopped coarsely
½ teaspoon ground cinnamon

1 Blend or process ingredients, in batches, until smooth.

serves 4
per serving 0.9g fat; 638kJ (152 cal); 0.1g saturated fat; 3.7g fibre; 29g carbohydrate; low GI

buckwheat pancakes with lemon cream

PREPARATION TIME 10 MINUTES **COOKING TIME** 10 MINUTES

½ cup (75g) buckwheat flour
¼ cup (35g) wholemeal
   self-raising flour
1½ teaspoons baking powder
½ teaspoon ground cinnamon
2 egg whites
¾ cup (180ml) no-fat milk
1 tablespoon lemon juice
2 tablespoons maple syrup
20g low-fat dairy-free
   spread, melted
2 teaspoons coarsely grated
   lemon rind
LEMON CREAM
⅓ cup (80g) light sour cream
1 teaspoon finely grated
   lemon rind
1 teaspoon caster sugar

1 Sift flours, baking powder and cinnamon into medium bowl; gradually whisk in combined egg white, milk, juice and syrup. Stir spread into batter.

2 Pour ¼ cup batter into heated small lightly greased non-stick frying pan; cook about 2 minutes or until bubbles appear on the surface. Turn pancake; cook until lightly browned on other side. Remove from pan; cover to keep warm. Repeat with remaining batter. Serve with lemon cream; top with rind.
lemon cream Place ingredients in small bowl; stir until combined.

serves 4
per serving 6g fat; 837kJ (200 cal); 3.3g saturated fat; 3.2g fibre; 28.5g carbohydrate; medium GI

breakfast with the lot

PREPARATION TIME 10 MINUTES **COOKING TIME** 25 MINUTES

2 large egg tomatoes (180g), quartered
4 eggs
4 slices multigrain bread
60g light ham
50g baby spinach leaves

1 Preheat oven to hot. Line oven tray with baking paper.
2 Place tomato, cut-side up, on prepared tray; roast, uncovered,
in hot oven about 25 minutes or until softened and lightly browned.
3 Meanwhile, place enough water in a large shallow non-stick frying pan
to come halfway up the side; bring to a boil. Break eggs, one at a time,
into small bowl, sliding each into pan; allow water to return to a boil.
Cover pan, turn off heat; stand about 4 minutes or until a light film
of egg white has set over each yolk.
4 Toast bread slices until lightly browned both sides.
5 Using an egg slide, remove eggs, one at a time, from pan; place egg,
still on slide, on absorbent-paper-lined saucer to blot up any poaching
liquid. Serve toast topped with ham, spinach, egg then tomato.

serves 4
per serving 7g fat; 680kJ (160 cal); 2g saturated fat;
2.1g fibre; 12g carbohydrate; medium GI

Egg tomatoes, also known as roma or
plum tomatoes, are small and oval in
shape; they are often used in Italian dishes

morning trifles

PREPARATION TIME 20 MINUTES

You need about 5 passionfruit for this recipe.

⅓ cup (20g) All-Bran
⅓ cup (20g) Special K
⅓ cup (20g) puffed wheat
250g strawberries, hulled
1 cup (280g) low-fat
  vanilla yogurt
⅓ cup (80ml) passionfruit pulp

1 Combine cereals in small bowl.
2 Cut six strawberries in half; reserve. Slice remaining strawberries thinly.
3 Divide half of the cereal mixture among four 1-cup (250ml) serving bowls; divide half of the yogurt, all the strawberry slices and half of the passionfruit pulp among bowls. Continue layering with remaining cereal and yogurt; top with reserved strawberry halves and remaining passionfruit pulp.

serves 4
per serving 0.7g fat; 527kJ (126 cal); 0.1g saturated fat; 6.4g fibre; 20.4g carbohydrate; low GI

untoasted muesli

PREPARATION TIME 10 MINUTES

2 cups (180g) rolled oats

½ cup (35g) All-Bran

1 tablespoon sunflower
   seed kernels

⅓ cup (55g) sultanas

¼ cup (35g) finely chopped
   dried apricots

½ cup (80g) finely chopped
   seeded dried dates

3 cups (750ml) no-fat milk

½ cup (140g) low-fat yogurt

1 Combine rolled oats, All-Bran, sunflower seed
   kernels and dried fruit in large bowl.

2 Divide muesli and milk among serving bowls.
   Top with yogurt.

serves 6
per serving 4.1g fat; 1132kJ (270 cal);
0.7g saturated fat; 6.2g fibre;
47.3g carbohydrate; medium GI
tip You can use fruit juice, such as apple juice,
instead of the milk, if you prefer.

egg-white omelette

PREPARATION TIME 10 MINUTES **COOKING TIME** 15 MINUTES

150g light ham
200g button mushrooms, sliced thinly
12 egg whites
¼ cup finely chopped fresh chives
2 medium tomatoes (380g), chopped coarsely
½ cup (45g) coarsely grated low-fat cheddar cheese
8 slices wholemeal bread

1　Trim and discard any fat from ham; cut into thin strips. Cook ham in heated large non-stick frying pan, stirring, until lightly browned. Remove from pan. Cook mushrooms in same pan, stirring, until lightly browned.

2　Using electric mixer, beat 3 of the egg whites in small bowl until soft peaks form; fold in a quarter of the chives. Preheat grill. Pour egg-white mixture into heated lightly oiled non-stick 20cm frying pan; cook, uncovered, over low heat until just browned underneath. Place pan under preheated grill; cook until top just sets. Place a quarter of the tomato on one half of the omelette; return to grill, cook until tomato is hot and top is lightly browned. Gently place a quarter of each of the cheese, ham and mushroom on tomato half of omelette; fold over to enclose filling. Carefully transfer omelette to serving plate; cover to keep warm.

3　Repeat step 2 with remaining egg whites, chives and fillings.

4　Toast bread until lightly browned both sides. Serve omelettes with toast.

serves 4
per serving　6.3g fat; 1268kJ (303 cal); 1.7g saturated fat; 7.4g fibre; 33.1g carbohydrate; low GI

Button mushrooms have a mild earthy flavour and can be eaten raw or cooked

strawberry hotcakes with blueberry sauce

PREPARATION TIME 15 MINUTES **COOKING TIME** 20 MINUTES

1 egg, separated
2 egg whites, extra
½ cup (125ml) apple sauce
1 teaspoon vanilla essence
2 cups (560g) low-fat yogurt
1¾ cups (280g) wholemeal self-raising flour
250g strawberries, hulled, chopped coarsely
BLUEBERRY SAUCE
150g blueberries, chopped coarsely
2 tablespoons sugar
1 tablespoon water

1 Using electric mixer, beat all egg whites in small bowl until soft peaks form.
2 Meanwhile, combine egg yolk, apple sauce, essence, yogurt, flour and strawberries in large bowl; fold in egg whites.
3 Pour ¼ cup batter into heated large lightly greased non-stick frying pan; using spatula, spread batter to shape into a round. Cook, over low heat, about 2 minutes or until bubbles appear on the surface. Turn hotcake; cook until lightly browned on other side. Remove from pan; cover to keep warm. Repeat with remaining batter. Serve with blueberry sauce.
blueberry sauce Combine ingredients in small saucepan; bring to a boil, stirring constantly. Reduce heat; simmer 2 minutes. Remove from heat; cool. Blend or process blueberry mixture until smooth.

serves 4
per serving 3.4g fat; 1639kJ (391 cal); 0.8g saturated fat; 10g fibre; 67g carbohydrate; medium GI

With a juicy centre and sweet taste, blueberries have easily become one of our year-round all-time-favourite berries

snacks & light meals

kumara and coriander soup

PREPARATION TIME 10 MINUTES **COOKING TIME** 35 MINUTES

1 teaspoon canola oil
2 medium leeks (700g), chopped coarsely
3 cloves garlic, quartered
2 medium kumara (800g), chopped coarsely
1 litre (4 cups) chicken stock
⅔ cup (160ml) light evaporated milk
⅓ cup finely chopped fresh coriander

1 Heat oil in large saucepan; cook leek and garlic, stirring, until leek softens. Add kumara; cook, stirring, 5 minutes. Add stock; bring to a boil. Reduce heat; simmer, covered, about 20 minutes or until kumara softens.
2 Blend or process soup, in batches, until smooth; return soup to same cleaned pan. Simmer, uncovered, until soup thickens slightly. Stir in evaporated milk and coriander; stir over heat, without boiling, until heated through. Top with fresh coriander leaves, if desired.

serves 4
per serving 2.9g fat; 880kJ (210 cal); 0.7g saturated fat; 6.8g fibre; 34.6g carbohydrate; low GI

beetroot soup

1 teaspoon olive oil

1 small brown onion (80g),
   chopped coarsely

1 clove garlic, crushed

3 medium beetroot (500g),
   trimmed, chopped coarsely

1 medium apple (150g), cored,
   chopped coarsely

1 litre (4 cups) vegetable stock

½ cup (125ml) water

¼ cup (60ml) lemon juice

¼ teaspoon Tabasco sauce

½ lebanese cucumber (65g),
   seeded, chopped finely

½ small red onion (50g),
   chopped finely

1 tablespoon light sour cream

1 Heat oil in large saucepan;
cook onion and garlic, stirring,
until onion softens. Add beetroot,
apple, stock and the water;
bring to a boil. Reduce heat;
simmer, covered, about
20 minutes or until beetroot
is tender, stirring occasionally.

2 Blend or process soup, in
batches, until smooth. Stir in
juice and sauce; refrigerate,
covered, until cold.

3 Serve chilled soup topped with
combined remaining ingredients.

serves 4
per serving 3.4g fat; 519kJ
(124 cal); 1.4g saturated fat;
4.7g fibre; 17.2g carbohydrate;
medium GI

oven-roasted potato wedges with tomato relish

PREPARATION TIME 15 MINUTES **COOKING TIME** 40 MINUTES

1kg large new potatoes
vegetable-oil spray
1 teaspoon salt
1 teaspoon freshly ground
   black pepper
4 medium tomatoes (760g),
   chopped finely
1 small brown onion (80g),
   chopped finely
2 tablespoons brown sugar
2 tablespoons red wine vinegar
1 teaspoon mustard powder

1 Preheat oven to very hot.
2 Halve potatoes lengthways; cut
   each half into wedges. Place
   wedges, in single layer, in large
   shallow baking dish; spray with
   oil, sprinkle with salt and pepper.
   Bake, uncovered, in very hot oven
   about 30 minutes or until browned
   and crisp, turning occasionally.
3 Meanwhile, heat tomato, onion,
   sugar, vinegar and mustard in
   medium saucepan; bring to
   a boil. Reduce heat; simmer,
   uncovered, about 30 minutes
   or until relish thickens. Serve
   potato wedges with relish.

serves 6
per serving 1.2g fat; 954kJ
(228 cal); 0.1g saturated fat;
4.5g fibre; 29.5g carbohydrate;
high GI

tofu cakes with sweet chilli dipping sauce

PREPARATION TIME 15 MINUTES (PLUS STANDING TIME) **COOKING TIME** 15 MINUTES

You need to cook about ⅓ cup basmati rice for this recipe.

300g fresh firm tofu
1 cup (150g) cooked basmati rice
3 teaspoons red curry paste
2 green onions, chopped finely
1 tablespoon coarsely chopped fresh coriander
1 egg, beaten lightly
SWEET CHILLI DIPPING SAUCE
¼ cup (60ml) white vinegar
½ cup (110g) caster sugar
½ teaspoon salt
¾ cup (180ml) water
½ small red onion (50g), chopped finely
½ small carrot (35g), chopped finely
½ small lebanese cucumber (65g), seeded, chopped finely
2 tablespoons coarsely chopped fresh coriander
⅓ cup (80ml) sweet chilli sauce

1 Press tofu between two chopping boards or trays, place weight
   on top; elevate boards slightly to allow tofu liquid to drain away.
   Stand 20 minutes; chop coarsely. Blend or process tofu until smooth.
2 Preheat oven to moderately hot; line oven tray with baking paper.
3 Combine tofu in medium bowl with rice, paste, onion, coriander and egg.
4 Shape level tablespoons of the tofu mixture into rounds; place on
   oven tray. Bake, uncovered, in moderately hot oven about 10 minutes
   or until lightly browned and heated through. Serve tofu cakes with
   sweet chilli dipping sauce.
   sweet chilli dipping sauce Place vinegar, sugar, salt and the water
   in small saucepan; bring to a boil. Boil, stirring, about 2 minutes or
   until sugar dissolves. Pour vinegar mixture over remaining ingredients
   in medium heatproof bowl; stir to combine.

makes 20 tofu cakes
per cake 1.7g fat; 326kJ (78 cal); 0.3g saturated fat;
0.8g fibre; 12.9g carbohydrate; medium GI

herbed chicken rice paper rolls

PREPARATION TIME 30 MINUTES (PLUS REFRIGERATION TIME) **COOKING TIME** 5 MINUTES

200g chicken tenderloins
1 tablespoon coarsely
   chopped fresh basil
1 tablespoon coarsely
   chopped fresh mint
1 tablespoon white
   wine vinegar
1 medium carrot (120g)
½ medium red capsicum (100g)
½ lebanese cucumber
   (65g), seeded
16cm-square rice paper sheets
2 tablespoons finely chopped
   roasted unsalted peanuts
1 tablespoon lime juice
2 tablespoons soy sauce
½ teaspoon grated fresh ginger

1 Combine chicken, basil, mint and vinegar in medium bowl, cover; refrigerate at least 10 minutes.
2 Meanwhile, cut carrot, capsicum and cucumber into thin strips.
3 Cook chicken on heated lightly oiled grill plate (or grill or barbecue) until lightly browned all over and cooked through. Stand 5 minutes; slice thinly.
4 Using hands, dip rice paper sheets, one at a time, in medium bowl of warm water until just softened; dry carefully with absorbent paper. Divide chicken, carrot, capsicum and cucumber along centre of each rice paper sheet; scatter peanuts over filling. Roll rice paper sheets to enclose filling, folding in sides after first complete turn of roll. Serve rolls with dipping sauce made with combined remaining ingredients.

serves 4
per serving 6.5g fat; 891kJ (213 cal); 1.4g saturated fat; 2.1g fibre; 22.5g carbohydrate; low GI

Mesclun is a gourmet salad mix consisting of young lettuce and baby spinach leaves, mizuna and curly endive

niçoise salad

PREPARATION TIME 15 MINUTES **COOKING TIME** 5 MINUTES

100g green beans, trimmed
2 x 180g cans tuna in
    springwater, drained
1 small red onion (100g),
    sliced thinly
2 green onions, sliced thinly
250g cherry tomatoes, halved
100g mesclun
2 teaspoons finely grated
    lemon rind
½ cup (125ml) lemon juice
1 tablespoon
    wholegrain mustard
2 cloves garlic, crushed
2 teaspoons sugar

1 Boil, steam or microwave
   beans until just tender; cool.
   Cut beans in half.
2 Combine beans with tuna,
   onions, tomato and mesclun
   in large bowl.
3 Whisk remaining ingredients
   in small bowl; add to salad,
   toss gently to combine.

serves 4
per serving 2.3g fat; 568kJ
(136 cal); 0.7g saturated fat;
3.1g fibre; 7.3g carbohydrate;
low GI

lamb and tabbouleh wrap

PREPARATION TIME 35 MINUTES **COOKING TIME** 10 MINUTES

Sumac, a purple-red astringent spice, can be teamed with almost anything – from fish to meat. It is also great sprinkled over vegetables. You can find sumac at any Middle-Eastern food store.

1 cup (250ml) water
½ cup (80g) burghul
300g can chickpeas, drained, rinsed
⅓ cup (95g) low-fat yogurt
1 teaspoon finely grated lemon rind
1 tablespoon lemon juice
3 green onions, sliced thinly
2 medium tomatoes (380g), seeded, chopped finely
1 lebanese cucumber (130g), seeded, chopped finely
1 cup coarsely chopped fresh flat-leaf parsley
½ cup coarsely chopped fresh mint
1 tablespoon lemon juice, extra
250g lean lamb strips
2 tablespoons sumac
8 slices lavash bread

1 Combine the water and burghul in small bowl; stand 30 minutes. Drain; squeeze burghul with hands to remove excess water.
2 Meanwhile, blend or process chickpeas, yogurt, rind and juice until hummus is smooth.
3 Combine burghul in large bowl with onion, tomato, cucumber and herbs; add extra juice, toss gently until tabbouleh is combined.
4 Toss lamb in sumac; cook, in batches, on heated lightly oiled grill plate (or grill or barbecue) until browned both sides and cooked as desired.
5 Just before serving, spread hummus equally over half of each slice of the bread, top with equal amounts of lamb and tabbouleh; roll to enclose filling. Cut into pieces, if desired, to serve.

makes 8 wraps
per wrap 4.9g fat; 1304kJ (311 cal); 1.4g saturated fat; 7.7g fibre; 48.4g carbohydrate; medium GI

rice and chickpea salad

PREPARATION TIME 15 MINUTES **COOKING TIME** 10 MINUTES (PLUS STANDING TIME)

Doongara rice has a lower glycaemic index than most other types of rice, and can be found at your local supermarket.

1 cup (200g) doongara rice
1¾ cups (430ml) water
300g can chickpeas,
   rinsed, drained
¼ cup (40g) sultanas
¼ cup (35g) dried apricots,
   chopped finely
2 green onions, sliced thinly
2 tablespoons toasted
   pine nuts
BALSAMIC ORANGE
DRESSING
1 teaspoon finely grated
   orange rind
⅓ cup (80ml) orange juice
1 tablespoon balsamic vinegar
1 clove garlic, crushed
1 teaspoon grated fresh ginger

1 Combine rice and the water in medium heavy-based saucepan; bring to a boil. Reduce heat; simmer, covered, about 8 minutes or until rice is tender. Remove from heat; stand, covered, 10 minutes. Fluff rice with fork; cool then refrigerate, covered, until cold.
2 Combine rice with remaining ingredients in large bowl; add balsamic orange dressing, toss gently to combine.
   balsamic orange dressing
   Combine ingredients in screw-topped jar; shake well.

serves 6
per serving 4.3g fat; 929kJ (222 cal); 0.2g saturated fat; 2.1g fibre; 26.7g carbohydrate; low GI

Also known as garbanzos, hummus or channa, chickpeas are often used in Latin and Mediterranean cooking

curried chicken and zucchini soup

PREPARATION TIME 10 MINUTES **COOKING TIME** 25 MINUTES

Doongara, the Aboriginal word for white lightning, is a gluten-free rice that can be found at your local supermarket.

1 tablespoon low-fat
  dairy-free spread
1 medium brown onion (150g),
  chopped finely
1 clove garlic, crushed
1 teaspoon curry powder
½ cup (100g) doongara rice
340g chicken breast fillets,
  sliced thinly
2 cups (500ml) water
1 litre (4 cups) chicken stock
4 medium zucchini,
  grated coarsely

1 Melt spread in large saucepan; cook onion and garlic, stirring, until onion softens. Add curry powder; cook, stirring, until mixture is fragrant.

2 Add rice and chicken; cook, stirring, 2 minutes. Add the water and stock; bring to a boil. Reduce heat; simmer, covered, 10 minutes. Add zucchini; cook, stirring, about 5 minutes or until chicken is cooked through.

serves 4
per serving 6.7g fat; 1098kJ (262 cal); 2.1g saturated fat; 2.7g fibre; 25.7g carbohydrate; medium GI

chilli and lime chicken salad

PREPARATION TIME 20 MINUTES (PLUS COOLING TIME) **COOKING TIME** 10 MINUTES

1 cup (250ml) water
1 cup (250ml) chicken stock
340g chicken breast fillets
1 small carrot (70g)
1 small red capsicum (150g), sliced thinly
½ small chinese cabbage (200g), shredded finely
2 green onions, chopped finely
¾ cup (60g) bean sprouts
½ cup firmly packed fresh coriander leaves
100g watercress, trimmed
CHILLI LIME DRESSING
¼ cup (60ml) lime juice
2 tablespoons sweet chilli sauce
1 clove garlic, crushed
1 tablespoon oyster sauce
1 teaspoon sesame oil

1 Bring the water and stock to a boil in large saucepan. Reduce heat; add chicken, simmer about 10 minutes or until chicken is cooked through. Allow chicken to cool in cooking liquid before draining. Discard liquid; slice chicken thinly.
2 Meanwhile, halve carrot crossways, cut each half into 2mm-wide lengths; cut lengths into matchstick-thin strips.
3 Place chicken and carrot in large bowl with capsicum, cabbage, onion, sprouts, coriander and watercress; add chilli lime dressing, toss to combine.
chilli lime dressing Combine ingredients in screw-topped jar; shake well.

serves 4
per serving 6.7g fat; 751kJ (179 cal); 1.8g saturated fat; 4g fibre; 7.2g carbohydrate; medium GI

The delectable yet low-fat Thai sweet chilli sauce is fantastic in dressings, dips or stir-fries

swiss brown mushroom and barley soup

PREPARATION TIME 10 MINUTES **COOKING TIME** 55 MINUTES

300g swiss brown
  mushrooms, quartered
1 clove garlic, crushed
2 teaspoons soy sauce
2 teaspoons water
1 small brown onion (80g),
  chopped finely
1 litre (4 cups) chicken stock
1 litre (4 cups) water, extra
½ cup (100g) pearl barley
1 untrimmed stick celery (150g),
  chopped coarsely
2 small carrots (140g),
  chopped coarsely
½ teaspoon freshly ground
  black pepper

1 Cook mushrooms, garlic, soy
  sauce and the water in heated
  large non-stick frying pan until
  mushrooms soften.
2 Cook onion in heated lightly
  oiled large saucepan, stirring,
  until softened. Add stock and
  the extra water; bring to a boil.
  Add barley, reduce heat; simmer,
  covered, 30 minutes.
3 Add mushroom mixture to
  saucepan with remaining
  ingredients; cook, uncovered,
  about 20 minutes or until barley
  and vegetables are tender.

serves 4
per serving 2.7g fat; 607kJ
(145kJ); 0.7g saturated fat;
6.4g fibre; 21.7g carbohydrate;
medium GI

chicken tikka wrap

PREPARATION TIME 20 MINUTES (PLUS REFRIGERATION TIME) **COOKING TIME** 15 MINUTES

2 single chicken breast
  fillets (340g)
1 tablespoon tikka masala
  curry paste
2½ cups (700g) low-fat yogurt
2 lebanese cucumbers (260g),
  seeded, chopped finely
⅓ cup coarsely chopped
  fresh mint
1 small red onion (100g),
  chopped finely
4 large pitta
100g mesclun

1 Cut each chicken fillet in half
   horizontally. Combine chicken
   in large bowl with paste and
   2 tablespoons of yogurt, cover;
   refrigerate 3 hours or overnight.
2 Cook chicken, in batches, on
   heated lightly oiled grill plate (or
   grill or barbecue) until browned
   all over and cooked through.
   Stand 5 minutes; slice thinly.
3 Meanwhile, combine cucumber,
   mint, onion and remaining yogurt
   in medium bowl.
4 Just before serving, spread
   yogurt mixture over whole of
   each piece of bread; top with
   equal amounts of mesclun then
   chicken. Roll to enclose filling.

serves 4
per serving 6.3g fat; 1248kJ
(298 cal); 1.7g saturated fat;
2.9g fibre; 25.3g carbohydrate;
medium GI

beef and bean tacos

PREPARATION TIME 15 MINUTES **COOKING TIME** 20 MINUTES

1 clove garlic, crushed
80g lean beef mince
½ teaspoon chilli powder
¼ teaspoon ground cumin
300g can kidney beans,
  rinsed, drained
2 tablespoons tomato paste
½ cup (125ml) water
1 medium tomato (190g),
  chopped coarsely
4 taco shells
¼ small iceberg lettuce,
  shredded finely
SALSA CRUDA
½ lebanese cucumber (65g),
  seeded, chopped finely
½ small red onion (40g),
  chopped finely
1 small tomato (130g), seeded,
  chopped finely
1 teaspoon mild chilli sauce

1 Preheat oven to moderate.
2 Heat large lightly oiled non-stick frying pan; cook garlic and beef,
   stirring, until beef is browned all over. Add chilli, cumin, beans, paste,
   the water and tomato; cook, covered, over low heat about 15 minutes
   or until mixture thickens slightly.
3 Meanwhile, toast taco shells, upside-down and uncovered, on oven tray
   in moderate oven for 5 minutes.
4 Just before serving, fill taco shells with beef mixture, lettuce and salsa cruda.
   salsa cruda Combine ingredients in small bowl.

serves 4
per serving 4.6g fat; 654kJ (156 cal); 1g saturated fat;
6.8g fibre; 18.4g carbohydrate; medium GI

roasted ratatouille with rye toast

PREPARATION TIME 15 MINUTES **COOKING TIME** 20 MINUTES

4 baby eggplants (240g),
   chopped coarsely
3 small green zucchini (270g),
   chopped coarsely
100g button mushrooms,
   chopped coarsely
250g cherry tomatoes, halved
1 small leek (200g),
   chopped coarsely
2 cloves garlic, crushed
1 tablespoon olive oil
½ cup coarsely chopped
   fresh basil
1 tablespoon finely chopped
   fresh oregano
2 tablespoons balsamic vinegar
4 thick slices dark rye
   bread, toasted

1 Preheat oven to hot.
2 Combine eggplant, zucchini,
   mushrooms, tomato, leek, garlic
   and oil in large shallow baking
   dish; roast, uncovered, in hot
   oven, stirring occasionally,
   about 20 minutes or until
   vegetables are tender.
3 Stir basil, oregano and vinegar
   into ratatouille. Serve warm
   on rye bread.

serves 4
per serving 6.2g fat; 766kJ
(183 cal); 0.8g saturated fat;
8.1g fibre; 24.2g carbohydrate;
high GI

mains

rosemary, brie and sun-dried tomato chicken on corn mash

PREPARATION TIME 30 MINUTES **COOKING TIME** 15 MINUTES

30g sun-dried tomatoes, chopped finely
1 tablespoon finely chopped fresh rosemary
4 single chicken breast fillets (680g)
60g firm brie, quartered
1kg medium new potatoes, quartered
2 cloves garlic, crushed
2 tablespoons no-fat milk
2 tablespoons light sour cream
310g can creamed corn

tips If sun-dried tomatoes are too dry, reconstitute in hot water; drain before mixing with the rosemary. You can substitute the corn with 125g of wilted baby spinach leaves, if desired.

serving suggestion A crisp mixed-leaf salad dressed with a splash of vinaigrette suits this main course perfectly.

1 Combine tomato and rosemary in small bowl.
2 Using small sharp knife, slit a pocket in one side of each fillet, taking care not to cut all the way through. Divide tomato mixture and brie among pockets; secure openings with toothpicks.
3 Cook chicken on heated lightly oiled grill plate (or grill or barbecue) until browned both sides and cooked through; cover to keep warm.
4 Meanwhile, boil, steam or microwave potato until tender; drain. Mash potato in large bowl with garlic, milk and sour cream; fold in corn. Serve chicken with mash.

serves 4
per serving 15g fat; 2124kJ (508 cal); 6g saturated fat; 7.5g fibre; 44.5g carbohydrate; high GI

linguine with lamb, asparagus and gremolata

PREPARATION TIME 20 MINUTES **COOKING TIME** 15 MINUTES

375g linguine
375g lamb fillets
500g asparagus, trimmed,
    chopped coarsely
⅓ cup finely grated lemon rind
4 cloves garlic, crushed
1 cup coarsely chopped fresh
    flat-leaf parsley
½ cup (125ml) lemon juice
8 green onions, sliced thinly
1 tablespoon olive oil

1 Cook pasta in large saucepan
   of boiling water until just tender;
   drain. Place in large bowl; cover
   to keep warm.
2 Meanwhile, cook lamb on heated
   lightly oiled grill plate (or grill or
   barbecue) until browned all over
   and cooked as desired. Cover;
   stand 5 minutes, slice thinly.
3 Boil, steam or microwave
   asparagus until just tender; drain.
4 Combine remaining ingredients
   in small bowl; pour over pasta.
   Add lamb and asparagus; toss
   gently to combine.

serves 6
per serving 6.2g fat; 1382kJ
(330 cal); 1g saturated fat;
2.9g fibre; 19.8g carbohydrate;
low GI

tip This recipe is good served
warm or at room temperature.
If not serving immediately, do not
toss the ingredients together or
the pasta will absorb the dressing.

oven-steamed ocean trout

PREPARATION TIME 10 MINUTES **COOKING TIME** 15 MINUTES

4 x 200g ocean trout fillets
2 tablespoons lemon juice
1 tablespoon drained capers,
  chopped coarsely
2 teaspoons coarsely
  chopped fresh dill
1.2kg large new potatoes,
  sliced thickly

1 Preheat oven to moderately hot.
2 Place each fillet on a square of
foil large enough to completely
enclose fish; top each fillet with
equal amounts of juice, capers
and dill. Gather corners of foil
squares together above fish,
twist to close securely.
3 Place parcels on oven tray; cook
in moderately hot oven about
15 minutes or until fish is cooked
as desired. Unwrap and remove
fish from foil before serving.
4 Meanwhile, boil, steam or
microwave potato until tender.
Serve fish with potato.

serves 4
per serving 7.9g fat; 1751kJ
(418 cal); 1.8g saturated fat;
5.8g fibre; 39g carbohydrate;
high GI

tip Use tweezers to remove
any bones from fish.
serving suggestion Accompany
trout with mixed salad leaves.

Rinse and drain capers
before using to rid them of
excess salt or brine

crisp-skinned snapper with stir-fried vegetables and black beans

PREPARATION TIME 15 MINUTES **COOKING TIME** 10 MINUTES

½ teaspoon sea salt

1 teaspoon coarsely ground black pepper

4 x 200g snapper fillets

1 teaspoon sesame oil

1 large brown onion (200g), cut into thin wedges

1 clove garlic, crushed

1 teaspoon grated fresh ginger

1 tablespoon salted black beans, rinsed, drained

1 medium green capsicum (200g), chopped coarsely

1 medium red capsicum (200g), chopped coarsely

6 green onions, sliced thickly

100g snow peas

100g broccolini, chopped coarsely

½ cup (125ml) water

¼ cup (60ml) oyster sauce

2 tablespoons lemon juice

500g baby bok choy, chopped coarsely

1 cup (80g) bean sprouts

tips Broccolini, a cross between broccoli and Chinese kale, is milder and sweeter than broccoli. Each long stem is topped by a loose floret that closely resembles broccoli; from floret to stem, broccolini is completely edible. Substitute chinese broccoli (gai larn) for the broccolini in this recipe, if you prefer.

serving suggestion Serve steamed doongarra rice with this dish; a small bowl of finely chopped red chilli in soy sauce can be passed to add a bit of zip to the fish.

1 Combine salt and pepper in small bowl; rub into skin side of each fillet. Cook fish, skin-side down, on heated lightly oiled grill plate (or grill or barbecue) until browned and crisp; turn, cook until browned and cooked as desired. Cover to keep warm.

2 Heat oil in wok or large frying pan; stir-fry brown onion, garlic and ginger until onion softens. Add beans; stir-fry 1 minute. Add capsicums, green onion, snow peas and broccolini; stir-fry until vegetables are just tender.

3 Stir in the water, sauce and juice; cook, stirring, until mixture thickens slightly. Add bok choy and bean sprouts; stir-fry until heated through. Serve fish on vegetables.

serves 4

per serving 5.3g fat; 1223kJ (292 cal); 1.4g saturated fat; 5.4g fibre; 12.6g carbohydrate; low GI

fried rice

PREPARATION TIME 10 MINUTES **COOKING TIME** 10 MINUTES

Also known as "Clever Rice", doongara rice is a white, long-grain, Australian-grown rice that can be found at your local supermarket. You need to cook about 1½ cups of rice for this recipe.

2 teaspoons peanut oil
1 medium brown onion (150g), chopped coarsely
2 cloves garlic, crushed
2 teaspoons grated fresh ginger
300g lean pork mince
1 untrimmed stick celery (150g), sliced thickly
1 small red capsicum (150g), chopped coarsely
1 large zucchini (150g), chopped coarsely
4 cups (600g) cooked doongara rice
¾ cup (90g) frozen peas, thawed
¼ cup (60ml) soy sauce
2 green onions, sliced thinly

tip Cold rice, cooked the day before you intend to prepare the recipe, is best for this dish; the individual grains remain separate from one another and won't get mushy when reheated in the wok. Spread the cooked rice on a tray and allow to cool before covering and refrigerating overnight.

serving suggestion Try topping each serving with a just-fried egg garnished with freshly chopped red chilli. Pass the kecap manis so that everyone can spoon a little over the egg and rice.

1 Heat oil in wok or large non-stick frying pan; stir-fry brown onion, garlic and ginger until onion has just softened. Add pork; stir-fry until brown and cooked through.
2 Add celery, capsicum and zucchini; stir-fry until just tender. Add rice, peas and sauce; stir-fry until hot. Toss green onion through fried rice just before serving.

serves 4
per serving 8.2g fat; 1527kJ (365 cal); 2.4g saturated fat; 4.2g fibre; 19.6g carbohydrate; medium GI

Kecap manis, also spelt ketjap manis, is an Indonesian thick, sweet soy sauce that adds a great flavour to stir-fries

artichoke risotto

PREPARATION TIME 10 MINUTES **COOKING TIME** 25 MINUTES

While the short-grained arborio is traditionally used in a risotto, we chose to use the longer-grained doongara rice here because it has both a lower GI rating and is more amenable to being cooked with the liquids added all at once.

2 teaspoons olive oil
1 medium brown onion (150g), chopped finely
3 cloves garlic, crushed
6 green onions, sliced thinly
2 cups (400g) doongara rice
¾ cup (180ml) dry white wine
1½ cups (375ml) chicken stock
3 cups (750ml) water
400g can artichoke hearts, drained, sliced thinly
½ cup (40g) finely grated parmesan cheese

serving suggestion A salad of grape tomatoes, sliced fennel and a few fresh basil leaves suits this risotto perfectly.

1 Heat oil in large saucepan; cook brown onion, garlic and half of the green onion, stirring, until brown onion softens. Add rice, wine, stock and the water; bring to a boil. Reduce heat; simmer, covered, 15 minutes, stirring occasionally.
2 Stir in artichokes, cheese and remaining green onion; cook, stirring, about 5 minutes or until artichokes are heated through.

serves 6
per serving 4.5g fat; 1353kJ (323 cal); 1.2g saturated fat; 1.8g fibre; 37g carbohydrate; medium GI

Continue the Italian theme and serve the risotto with fresh slices of crusty ciabatta, if desired

lentil cottage pie

PREPARATION TIME 10 MINUTES **COOKING TIME** 45 MINUTES (PLUS STANDING TIME)

800g medium new potatoes, quartered

2 tablespoons low-fat dairy-free spread

1 medium brown onion (150g), chopped finely

1 clove garlic, crushed

415g can crushed tomatoes

1 cup (250ml) vegetable stock

1 cup (250ml) water

2 tablespoons tomato paste

⅓ cup (80ml) dry red wine

⅔ cup (130g) red lentils

1 medium carrot (120g), chopped finely

½ cup (60g) frozen peas, thawed

2 tablespoons worcestershire sauce

⅓ cup coarsely chopped fresh flat-leaf parsley

tip If you're not concerned with keeping the fat content of this dish low, you can stir ½ cup of finely grated parmesan cheese into the potato mash before baking the cottage pie.

serving suggestion Serve with a simple green salad, if desired.

1 Preheat oven to hot.

2 Boil, steam or microwave potato until tender; drain. Mash in large bowl with half of the spread.

3 Melt remaining spread in medium deep frying pan; cook onion and garlic, stirring, until onion softens. Add undrained tomatoes, stock, the water, paste, wine, lentils and carrot; bring to a boil. Reduce heat; simmer, uncovered, 15 minutes, stirring occasionally. Add peas, sauce and parsley; cook, uncovered, 5 minutes.

4 Spoon lentil mixture into shallow 1-litre (4 cup) ovenproof dish. Spread potato mash on top. Bake, uncovered, in hot oven 20 minutes. Stand pie 10 minutes before serving.

serves 4

per serving 7.2g fat; 1341kJ (320 cal); 1.2g saturated fat; 11.3g fibre; 45.1g carbohydrate; high GI

Silverbeet, also known as swiss chard or chard, is a leafy, dark green vegetable

silverbeet, mushroom and capsicum frittata

PREPARATION TIME 15 MINUTES **COOKING TIME** 45 MINUTES

500g silverbeet, trimmed, chopped coarsely
1 tablespoon low-fat dairy-free spread
1 medium brown onion (150g), chopped finely
2 cloves garlic, crushed
1 medium red capsicum (200g), chopped finely
2 trimmed sticks celery (150g), chopped finely
100g button mushrooms, sliced thinly
2 large carrots (360g), grated coarsely
¼ cup (40g) polenta
¼ cup coarsely chopped fresh basil
3 eggs, beaten lightly
3 egg whites, beaten lightly
⅓ cup (80ml) no-fat milk

tip This frittata is just as good eaten at room temperature as it is hot from the oven.
serving suggestion Serve frittata with a salad of mixed grape, cherry and teardrop tomatoes.

1 Preheat oven to moderate.
2 Line 20cm x 30cm lamington pan with baking paper.
3 Boil, steam or microwave silverbeet; drain on absorbent paper.
4 Melt spread in large deep frying pan; cook onion and garlic, stirring, until onion softens. Add capsicum, celery and mushrooms; cook, stirring, until vegetables just soften.
5 Stir silverbeet, carrot, polenta and basil into vegetable mixture. Remove from heat; cool 5 minutes. Add eggs, whites and milk; stir to combine. Spread frittata mixture into prepared pan; bake, uncovered, in moderate oven about 35 minutes or until lightly browned and firm to the touch.

serves 4
per serving 6.7g fat; 809kJ (193 cal); 1.6g saturated fat; 8.3g fibre; 19.3g carbohydrate; medium GI

herb-crusted lamb racks with kipfler potatoes and leek

PREPARATION TIME 25 MINUTES **COOKING TIME** 55 MINUTES (PLUS STANDING TIME)

4 x 3-cutlet racks of lamb (900g)
¼ cup (20g) fresh white breadcrumbs
1 tablespoon finely chopped fresh rosemary
1 tablespoon finely chopped fresh flat-leaf parsley
2 teaspoons finely chopped fresh thyme
3 cloves garlic, crushed
3 teaspoons bottled coriander pesto
1kg kipfler potatoes, halved lengthways
vegetable-oil spray
1 teaspoon sea salt
2 medium leeks (700g), trimmed
2 teaspoons low-fat dairy-free spread
¼ cup (60ml) chicken stock
¼ cup (60ml) dry white wine

tip Herbed breadcrumb mixture can be patted onto racks the day before serving. Cover and refrigerate overnight.
serving suggestion Mesclun with a lemon and rosemary-scented vinaigrette marries with this main course beautifully.

1 Preheat oven to moderately hot.
2 Remove any excess fat from lamb. Combine breadcrumbs, herbs, garlic and pesto in small bowl. Using hands, press breadcrumb mixture onto lamb racks, cover; refrigerate until required.
3 Place potato in large shallow baking dish; spray with oil, sprinkle with salt. Roast, uncovered, in moderately hot oven 20 minutes.
4 Place lamb on top of the potato; roast, uncovered, in moderately hot oven 10 minutes. Reduce heat to slow; cook about 20 minutes or until potato is tender and lamb is cooked as desired.
5 Meanwhile, cut leeks into 10cm lengths; slice thinly lengthways. Melt spread in large frying pan; cook leek, stirring, until leek softens. Stir in stock and wine; bring to a boil. Reduce heat; simmer, uncovered, until liquid reduces by half.
6 Stand lamb 5 minutes before cutting racks into cutlets; serve cutlets with potato and leek.

serves 4
per serving 13.7g fat; 1829kJ (437 cal); 5.6g saturated fat; 7.9g fibre; 40.1g carbohydrate; high GI

cajun-spiced fish with roasted corn salsa

PREPARATION TIME 15 MINUTES **COOKING TIME** 25 MINUTES

1 clove garlic, crushed

1 tablespoon low-fat dairy-free spread, melted

2 teaspoons sweet paprika

½ teaspoon ground cumin

1 teaspoon ground white pepper

¼ teaspoon cayenne pepper

4 x 200g firm white fish fillets

3 trimmed fresh corn cobs (750g)

1 small red onion (100g), chopped coarsely

1 medium avocado (250g), chopped coarsely

250g cherry tomatoes, halved

2 tablespoons lime juice

¼ cup coarsely chopped fresh coriander

tip We used blue-eye fillets for this recipe but you can use whichever firm white fish fillet you prefer.

serving suggestion A stack of warmed flour tortillas accompanies this flavoursome dish extremely well.

1 Preheat oven to hot.

2 Combine garlic and spread in small jug; combine spices in small bowl.

3 Place fish on oven tray, brush both sides with garlic mixture, sprinkle with combined spices. Roast, uncovered, in hot oven about 15 minutes or until browned both sides and cooked as desired.

4 Meanwhile, roast corn on heated lightly oiled grill plate (or grill or barbecue) until browned all over. When corn is just cool enough to handle, cut kernels from cobs with a small, sharp knife.

5 Combine corn kernels in medium bowl with remaining ingredients. Serve fish with salsa.

serves 4
per serving 15g fat; 1832kJ (438 cal); 3.4g saturated fat; 8.7g fibre; 26.1g carbohydrate; low GI

Serve the fish and salsa with tortillas warmed briefly in a microwave oven until they become pliable

tofu stir-fry

PREPARATION TIME 20 MINUTES (PLUS STANDING TIME) **COOKING TIME** 10 MINUTES

400g fresh firm tofu
400g fresh egg noodles
1 tablespoon sesame oil
2 cloves garlic, crushed
2 red thai chillies, seeded, sliced thinly
1 small red onion (100g), cut into wedges
1 medium red capsicum (200g), chopped coarsely
150g green beans, halved
200g swiss brown mushrooms, halved
4 green onions, sliced thinly
2 tablespoons soy sauce
2 tablespoons oyster sauce
1 tablespoon brown sugar

tip Some Asian supermarkets sell tofu already fried and cut into squares; while this will contain more fat than our oven-browned tofu, it also will shorten the preparation time for this dish.

1 Preheat oven to hot. Line oven tray with baking paper.
2 Press tofu between two chopping boards or trays, place weight on top; elevate boards slightly to allow tofu liquid to drain away. Stand 20 minutes; cut tofu into 2cm cubes. Place tofu on prepared oven tray; cook, uncovered, in hot oven about 25 minutes or until lightly browned.
3 Meanwhile, place noodles in large heatproof bowl, cover with boiling water; stand until just tender, separating noodles carefully with a fork. Drain; cover to keep warm.
4 Heat oil in wok or large frying pan; stir-fry garlic, chilli and red onion until onion softens. Add capsicum; stir-fry 2 minutes. Add beans and mushrooms; stir-fry until vegetables are just tender. Add tofu with green onion, sauces and sugar; stir-fry until sauce thickens slightly. Serve stir-fry tossed with noodles.

serves 4
per serving 11.3 g fat; 2474kJ (591 cal); 1.6g saturated fat; 8.3g fibre; 90.1g carbohydrate; low GI

Tofu, also known as bean curd, is the perfect substitute for meat when making vegetarian dishes

pork loin with couscous and apples

PREPARATION TIME 35 MINUTES **COOKING TIME** 1 HOUR

1 cup (200g) couscous
1 cup (250ml) boiling water
⅓ cup (55g) seeded prunes, chopped finely
1 tablespoon toasted pine nuts
2 tablespoons coarsely chopped fresh coriander
¼ cup coarsely chopped fresh flat-leaf parsley
500g rindless, boneless pork loin
2½ cups (625ml) alcoholic apple cider
2 medium apples (300g), peeled, cored, sliced thickly
1 large red onion (300g), cut into thick wedges
2 tablespoons brown sugar

tips We used Granny Smith apples in this recipe. To simplify making this recipe, ask your butcher to remove any excess fat and butterfly the pork for you.
serving suggestion A salad made of grated red cabbage, caraway seeds and sliced green onions, dressed in a cider vinaigrette, is the perfect accompaniment for this dish.

1 Preheat oven to moderately hot.
2 Combine couscous with the water in medium heatproof bowl, cover; stand about 5 minutes or until water is absorbed, fluffing with fork occasionally. Using fork, toss prunes, nuts, coriander and parsley into couscous.
3 Remove any excess fat from pork. Place pork on board, upside-down; slice through thickest part of pork horizontally, without cutting through at the other side. Open pork out to form one large piece; press 1 cup of the couscous mixture against loin along width of pork. Roll pork to enclose stuffing, securing with kitchen string at 2cm intervals.
4 Place rolled pork on rack in large shallow flameproof baking dish; pour 2 cups of the cider over pork. Roast, uncovered, in moderately hot oven about 50 minutes or until cooked through. Remove pork from baking dish; cover to keep warm.
5 Place remaining couscous mixture in small ovenproof dish; cook, covered, in moderately hot oven about 10 minutes or until heated through.
6 Meanwhile, heat pan juices in baking dish on top of stove; add remaining cider, apple, onion and sugar. Cook, stirring, until apple is just tender. Serve sliced pork with apple mixture and couscous.

serves 4
per serving 8.1g fat; 3044kJ (727 cal); 2g saturated fat; 4.6g fibre; 111.1g carbohydrate; low GI

beef, red wine and chilli casserole with polenta

PREPARATION TIME 15 MINUTES **COOKING TIME** 1 HOUR 45 MINUTES

2 teaspoons low-fat dairy-free spread
1.5kg lean beef chuck steak, cut into 3cm pieces
2 cloves garlic, crushed
3 red thai chillies, seeded, sliced thinly
2 teaspoons dijon mustard
1 large brown onion (200g), sliced thickly
2 medium tomatoes (380g), chopped coarsely
410g can tomato puree
¾ cup (180ml) dry red wine
½ cup (125ml) beef stock
1.125 litres (4½ cups) water
1 cup (170g) polenta
¼ cup (20g) finely grated parmesan cheese
2 tablespoons coarsely chopped fresh flat-leaf parsley

tip As long as the wine you use is good enough to drink with the meal, any dry red will suffice; however, in keeping with the Italian feel of this recipe, we used a Chianti.
serving suggestion Serve with baby rocket leaves sprinkled with flaked parmesan and a squeeze of lemon juice, if desired.

1 Melt spread in large saucepan; cook beef, in batches, until browned all over. Cook garlic, chilli, mustard and onion in same pan, stirring, until onion softens. Return beef to pan with tomato; cook, stirring, 2 minutes.
2 Add puree, wine, stock and ½ cup of the water to pan; bring to a boil. Reduce heat; simmer, covered, about 1 hour 30 minutes or until beef is tender, stirring occasionally.
3 Meanwhile, bring the remaining litre of water to a boil in medium saucepan. Add polenta; cook, stirring, over medium heat about 10 minutes or until thickened. Stir cheese into polenta.
4 Stir parsley into beef casserole just before serving with polenta.

serves 4
per serving 14.3g fat; 2058kJ (492 cal); 6.2g saturated fat; 3.7g fibre; 26.7g carbohydrate; low GI

tarragon chicken with carrot mash and leek

PREPARATION TIME 20 MINUTES (PLUS REFRIGERATION TIME) **COOKING TIME** 25 MINUTES

4 single chicken breast fillets (680g), sliced thickly
1 tablespoon finely chopped fresh tarragon
1 tablespoon wholegrain mustard
2 tablespoons low-fat dairy-free spread
2 large leeks (500g), trimmed, chopped finely
4 medium carrots (480g), chopped coarsely
1½ cups (375ml) chicken stock
pinch nutmeg

tips You need 12 bamboo skewers for this recipe; soak them in water for at least an hour before using to avoid them splintering or scorching. Do not puree the carrot mixture too far in advance because it could separate if left to stand too long.

serving suggestion Steamed green beans and a fresh baguette are good accompaniments for this main meal.

1 Thread equal amounts of chicken onto each of 12 skewers. Using fingers, press combined tarragon and mustard all over chicken, cover skewers; refrigerate 30 minutes.
2 Meanwhile, melt spread in large non-stick frying pan; cook leek, stirring, until softened. Cover to keep warm.
3 Preheat oven to moderately hot.
4 Boil or microwave carrot in chicken stock until just tender; drain in strainer over small bowl. Reserve ½ cup of the cooking liquid; discard the remainder. Blend or process carrot with nutmeg until pureed. Cover to keep warm.
5 Cook chicken and reserved liquid in large shallow baking dish, uncovered, in moderately hot oven about 15 minutes or until cooked through.
6 Divide carrot mash among serving plates; top with chicken and leek.

serves 4
per serving 13.9g fat; 1335kJ (319 cal); 1.4g saturated fat; 9g fibre; 76.8g carbohydrate; low GI

risoni marinara

PREPARATION TIME 15 MINUTES **COOKING TIME** 25 MINUTES

12 large uncooked prawns (600g)

12 small mussels (200g)

300g squid hoods

2 teaspoons olive oil

1 large brown onion (200g), chopped finely

2 cloves garlic, crushed

1 large red capsicum (350g), sliced thinly

375g risoni

1½ cups (375ml) water

1½ cups (375ml) chicken stock

½ cup (125ml) dry white wine

pinch saffron threads

1 cup (125g) frozen peas, thawed

1 large tomato (250g), seeded, sliced thinly

tip Risoni is a small, rice-sized pasta often used in Italian soups; orzo can be used instead of risoni for this recipe.

serving suggestion Salad caprese (basil leaves, bocconcini and sliced tomatoes) goes well with this paella-like one-course meal.

1 Shell and devein prawns, leaving tails intact. Scrub mussels; remove beards. Cut squid down centre to open out, score the inside in a diagonal pattern then cut into strips.

2 Heat oil in large saucepan; cook onion, garlic and capsicum, stirring, about 3 minutes or until onion softens. Add risoni; stir to coat in onion mixture.

3 Stir in the water, stock, wine and saffron; bring to a boil. Reduce heat; simmer, uncovered, until liquid is absorbed and risoni is just tender, stirring occasionally.

4 Add prawns, mussels, squid, peas and tomato; cook, covered, until prawns are changed in colour and mussels have opened (discard any that do not).

serves 4

per serving 6.5g fat; 2488kJ (594 cal); 1.4g saturated fat; 9g fibre; 76.8g carbohydrate; low GI

dhal with egg and eggplant

PREPARATION TIME 10 MINUTES **COOKING TIME** 1 HOUR

2 cups (400g) red lentils
2 teaspoons vegetable oil
1 medium brown onion (150g), chopped finely
1 clove garlic, crushed
2 teaspoons ground cumin
½ teaspoon cumin seeds
1 tablespoon tomato paste
1 litre (4 cups) water
2 cups (500ml) vegetable stock
1 large tomato (250g), chopped coarsely
3 baby eggplants (180g), chopped coarsely
4 hard-boiled eggs

tip Spoon a whole egg into each of four serving bowls then spoon dhal over the egg.
serving suggestion Serve with a bowl of steamed basmati rice.

1 Rinse lentils in large colander under cold water until water runs clear.
2 Heat oil in large heavy-based saucepan; cook onion, garlic, ground cumin, seeds and paste, stirring, 5 minutes. Add lentils with the water and stock; bring to a boil. Reduce heat; simmer, uncovered, about 40 minutes or until dhal mixture thickens slightly, stirring occasionally.
3 Add tomato and eggplant; simmer, uncovered, about 20 minutes or until dhal is thickened and eggplant is tender, stirring occasionally. Add whole eggs; stir gently until eggs are heated through.

serves 4
per serving 10.9g fat; 1698kJ (406 cal); 2.6g saturated fat; 16.7g fibre; 44.6g carbohydrate; low GI

A bowl of cucumber raita, made with low-fat plain yogurt and a hint of cumin, completes this Indian meal

singapore noodles

PREPARATION TIME 10 MINUTES **COOKING TIME** 20 MINUTES

250g rice vermicelli
4 eggs, beaten lightly
2 teaspoons vegetable oil
1 medium brown onion (150g), chopped coarsely
2 cloves garlic, crushed
2 teaspoons grated fresh ginger
150g baby bok choy, chopped coarsely
200g snow peas, halved
1 small red capsicum (150g), sliced thickly
2 tablespoons soy sauce
2 tablespoons oyster sauce
2 tablespoons sweet chilli sauce
1 cup loosely packed fresh coriander leaves
3 cups (240g) bean sprouts

serving suggestion Pass a platter of cucumber spears, quartered hard-boiled eggs, tomato wedges and sliced pawpaw to make this meal authentically Singaporean.

1 Place noodles in large heatproof bowl, cover with boiling water, stand until just tender; drain. Using scissors, cut noodles into 10cm lengths.

2 Heat lightly oiled wok or large non-stick frying pan; add half of the egg, swirling wok to form thin omelette. Remove omelette from wok; roll into cigar shape, cut into thin slices. Repeat with remaining egg.

3 Heat oil in same wok; stir-fry onion until soft. Add garlic and ginger; cook, stirring, 1 minute. Add bok choy, snow peas, capsicum and sauces; cook, stirring, until vegetables are just tender.

4 Add noodles and egg strips with coriander and sprouts to wok; toss gently to combine.

serves 4
per serving 9.9g fat; 1545kJ (369 cal); 2.1g saturated fat; 6.8g fibre; 52.5g carbohydrate; medium GI

satay beef and stir-fried vegetables with rice

PREPARATION TIME 20 MINUTES **COOKING TIME** 20 MINUTES

1 litre (4 cups) water
1 cup (200g) basmati rice
1 teaspoon peanut oil
500g lean beef topside, sliced thinly
1 large brown onion (200g), sliced thinly
1 clove garlic, crushed
2 teaspoons grated fresh ginger
2 red thai chillies, seeded, chopped finely
1 medium red capsicum (200g), chopped coarsely
1 medium green capsicum (200g), chopped coarsely
100g button mushrooms, halved
225g can bamboo shoots, drained
1 teaspoon curry powder
2 teaspoons cornflour
½ cup (125ml) chicken stock
¼ cup (65g) light smooth peanut butter
2 tablespoons oyster sauce
1 tablespoon unsalted, roasted, coarsely chopped peanuts

tip You can use sliced lamb fillets or sliced chicken thigh fillets instead of the beef, if you prefer.

1 Bring the water to a boil in large saucepan; stir in rice. Boil, uncovered, about 15 minutes or until rice is just tender. Drain, rinse under hot water; drain rice again, cover to keep warm.

2 Meanwhile, heat oil in wok or large non-stick frying pan; stir-fry beef, in batches, until browned all over.

3 Reheat meat juices in same wok; stir-fry onion and garlic until onion softens. Add ginger, chilli, capsicums, mushrooms, bamboo shoots and curry powder; stir-fry until vegetables are just tender.

4 Blend cornflour with stock in small jug; pour into wok, stir to combine with vegetable mixture. Return beef to wok with peanut butter and oyster sauce; bring to a boil, stirring, until sauce boils and thickens slightly and beef is cooked as desired. Stir in peanuts; serve with rice.

serves 4
per serving 14g fat; 2387kJ (570 cal); 2.3g saturated fat; 4g fibre; 70g carbohydrate; medium GI

pork vindaloo

PREPARATION TIME 15 MINUTES (PLUS STANDING TIME) **COOKING TIME** 50 MINUTES

2 large brown onions (400g), chopped coarsely
5 cloves garlic, quartered
1 teaspoon ground cardamom
½ teaspoon ground clove
1 teaspoon ground cinnamon
2 teaspoons ground cumin
2 teaspoons ground turmeric
2 teaspoons cracked black pepper
3 red thai chillies, quartered
2 teaspoons black mustard seeds
1 tablespoon grated fresh ginger
⅓ cup (80ml) white vinegar
1kg pork fillet, trimmed
1 tablespoon vegetable oil
1 large brown onion (200g), sliced thinly
2 tablespoons tamarind paste
2 large tomatoes (500g), chopped coarsely
2 cups (400g) jasmine rice

tips Vindaloo curry paste can be made up to a week ahead and kept, covered tightly, in the refrigerator. Making this dish a day ahead helps intensify the flavours.
serving suggestion Serve vindaloo with chopped cucumber and fresh pineapple, if desired.

1 Blend or process chopped onion, garlic, spices, chilli, seeds, ginger and vinegar to a smooth paste.
2 Trim any excess fat from pork; cut into 3cm pieces. Combine pork with a quarter of the curry paste in medium bowl; stir to coat pork all over. Cover; refrigerate 3 hours or overnight. Reserve remaining curry paste.
3 Heat oil in large saucepan; cook sliced onion, stirring, until just soft. Add reserved curry paste; cook, stirring, over low heat 5 minutes. Add pork; cook, stirring, about 5 minutes or until pork changes colour. Stir in tamarind paste and tomato; bring to a boil. Reduce heat; simmer, covered, about 40 minutes or until pork is tender and cooked through.
4 Meanwhile, cook rice in large saucepan of boiling water, uncovered, until just tender; drain. Serve curry on rice.

serves 4
per serving 11.6g fat; 3159kJ (755 cal); 2.7g saturated fat; 6.5g fibre; 94.4g carbohydrate; medium GI

grilled chicken with barley pilaf

PREPARATION TIME 10 MINUTES **COOKING TIME** 55 MINUTES

1 cup (215g) pearl barley
2 cups (500ml) water
2 cups (500ml) chicken stock
250g cherry tomatoes
150g yellow teardrop tomatoes
4 single chicken breast fillets (680g)
½ teaspoon coarsely ground black pepper
½ cup coarsely chopped fresh basil
2 green onions, sliced thinly
1 tablespoon dijon mustard

tip If tomatoes are too large, halve before roasting.

1 Preheat oven to hot.
2 Cook barley with the water and stock in medium saucepan, uncovered, over low heat, about 50 minutes or until most of the liquid is absorbed, stirring occasionally.
3 Meanwhile, roast tomatoes in hot oven on baking-paper-lined oven tray, uncovered, about 20 minutes or until just browned and softened.
4 Cook chicken on heated lightly oiled grill plate (or grill or barbecue) until browned both sides and cooked through.
5 Stir tomatoes, pepper, basil and onion gently into barley. Serve chicken, dolloped with mustard, with pilaf.

serves 4
per serving 11.3g fat; 1726kJ (412 cal); 3.4g saturated fat; 7.7g fibre; 34.2g carbohydrate; low GI

A salad of fresh baby spinach leaves drizzled with lemon juice goes well with this dish

roast baby vegetable pizza

PREPARATION TIME 15 MINUTES **COOKING TIME** 40 MINUTES

3 small zucchini (160g),
   sliced thinly
4 baby eggplants (240g),
   sliced thinly
10 cherry tomatoes, halved
1 baby fennel (130g),
   sliced thinly
100g button mushrooms,
   sliced thinly
⅔ cup (190g) bottled
   tomato pasta sauce
¼ cup coarsely chopped
   fresh basil
4 wholemeal pocket pitta
⅓ cup (40g) coarsely grated
   low-fat cheddar cheese

1 Preheat oven to hot.
2 Place zucchini, eggplant and
   tomato in lightly oiled shallow
   medium baking dish; roast,
   uncovered, 20 minutes.
3 Add fennel, mushrooms and all
   but 2 tablespoons of the pasta
   sauce to dish; roast, covered,
   10 minutes. Stir basil into
   vegetable mixture.
4 Divide reserved pasta sauce
   among bread pieces; top each
   with equal amounts of the
   vegetable mixture and cheese.
   Place on oven tray; cook,
   uncovered, in hot oven about
   10 minutes or until cheese melts
   and pizzas are heated through.

serves 4
per serving 2.9g fat; 1016kJ
(243 cal); 0.8g saturated fat;
8.1g fibre; 24.2g carbohydrate;
high GI

thai lamb salad

PREPARATION TIME 20 MINUTES (PLUS STANDING TIME) **COOKING TIME** 10 MINUTES

100g bean thread noodles
500g lamb fillets, trimmed
1 medium red onion (170g),
    sliced thinly
3 green onions, sliced thinly
1 cup (80g) bean sprouts
1 cup loosely packed fresh
    coriander leaves
1 cup loosely packed fresh
    mint leaves
1 cup loosely packed fresh
    vietnamese mint leaves
1 lebanese cucumber (130g),
    seeded, sliced thinly
2 red thai chillies, sliced thinly
200g cherry tomatoes, halved
2 cloves garlic, crushed
1 tablespoon finely chopped
    fresh lemon grass
⅓ cup (80ml) lime juice
1 tablespoon fish sauce
1 tablespoon soy sauce

1   Place noodles in medium
    heatproof bowl; cover with
    boiling water. Stand until just
    tender; drain. Rinse noodles
    under cold water; drain well.
2   Cook lamb on heated lightly oiled
    grill plate (or grill or barbecue) until
    browned and cooked as desired.
    Stand 5 minutes; slice thinly.
3   Meanwhile, combine onions,
    sprouts, herbs, cucumber, chilli
    and tomato in large bowl. Add
    lamb and combined remaining
    ingredients; toss to combine.
    Serve salad with noodles.

serves 4
per serving 4.9g fat; 997kJ
(238 cal); 2g saturated fat;
5.9g fibre; 18.3g carbohydrate;
low GI

desserts

tiramisu

PREPARATION TIME 20 MINUTES (PLUS REFRIGERATION TIME) **COOKING TIME** 25 MINUTES

3 eggs
½ cup (110g) caster sugar
¼ cup (40g) wholemeal
   self-raising flour
¼ cup (35g) white self-raising flour
¼ cup (35g) cornflour
1 teaspoon gelatine
1 tablespoon cold water
1½ cups (300g) low-fat ricotta cheese
¼ cup (60ml) no-fat milk
¼ cup (55g) caster sugar, extra
2 tablespoons instant coffee powder
2 tablespoons boiling water
⅓ cup (80ml) no-fat milk, extra
½ cup (125ml) coffee-flavoured liqueur
10g dark chocolate, grated finely

1 Preheat oven to moderate. Grease and line base
   of 22cm springform tin.
2 Using electric mixer, beat eggs in small bowl until thick
   and creamy. Gradually add sugar, beating until sugar
   dissolves. Fold triple-sifted flours into egg mixture until
   just combined. Spread into prepared tin.
3 Bake, uncovered, in moderate oven about 25 minutes.
   Turn onto wire rack to cool.
4 Meanwhile, sprinkle gelatine over the cold water in
   small heatproof jug; place jug in small pan of simmering
   water, stir until gelatine dissolves. Cool, 5 minutes.
5 Blend or process ricotta, milk and extra sugar until
   smooth. With motor operating, add gelatine mixture;
   process until combined. Dissolve coffee in the boiling
   water in small bowl; add extra milk and liqueur.
6 Cut cake in half horizontally. Return one cake half to
   same springform tin; brush half of the coffee mixture over
   cake; top with half of the ricotta mixture. Repeat with
   remaining cake half, coffee mixture and ricotta mixture.
7 Refrigerate tiramisu, covered, for at least 3 hours.
   Sprinkle top with grated chocolate just before serving.

serves 12
per serving 4.1g fat; 791kJ (189 cal); 2g saturated fat;
0.9g fibre; 28g carbohydrate; medium GI

Low-fat ricotta turns this
wicked dessert into a
deliciously light treat that
can be enjoyed by all

citrus rice pudding

Also labelled "Clever Rice", doongara rice is a white long-grain rice grown in Australia that can be found at your local supermarket. You need to cook about ½ cup of rice for this recipe.

2 cups (500ml) no-fat milk
1 vanilla bean, halved lengthways
1 teaspoon finely grated lemon rind
1 teaspoon finely grated lime rind
2 teaspoons finely grated orange rind
2 eggs
1 egg white
½ cup (110g) caster sugar
1½ cups (225g) cooked doongara rice
½ cup (125ml) low-fat cream

1 Preheat oven to moderately slow. Grease shallow oval 1.5-litre (6 cup) ovenproof dish.
2 Combine milk, vanilla bean and rinds in medium saucepan; bring to a boil. Remove from heat; stand, covered, 5 minutes.
3 Meanwhile, whisk eggs, egg white and sugar in medium bowl. Gradually whisk hot milk mixture into egg mixture; discard vanilla bean.
4 Spread rice into prepared dish; pour egg mixture carefully over rice. Place dish in large baking dish; add enough boiling water to baking dish to come halfway up side of pudding dish.
5 Bake, uncovered, in moderately slow oven about 1 hour or until set. Serve warm with cream.

serves 8
per serving 4.8g fat; 1094kJ (261 cal); 1.7g saturated fat; 0.2g fibre; 31.7g carbohydrate; medium GI

Vanilla beans contain a myriad tiny black seeds which impart their full flavour to both sweet and savoury dishes

florentines with berry ice-cream

PREPARATION TIME 10 MINUTES **COOKING TIME** 10 MINUTES

¼ cup (30g) toasted muesli

¼ cup (15g) bran flakes

¼ cup (40g) sultanas,
chopped coarsely

2 tablespoons finely chopped
dried apricots

1 tablespoon finely chopped
glacé cherries

1½ tablespoons flaked
almonds, toasted

¼ cup (60ml) light
condensed milk

1 tablespoon golden syrup

400g low-fat berry ice-cream

1 Preheat oven to moderate.
Grease two oven trays; line
each with baking paper.

2 Combine all ingredients except
ice-cream in medium bowl.

3 Drop tablespoons of the mixture
onto oven trays about 8cm
apart, spread into rounds.

4 Bake in moderate oven about
10 minutes or until florentines
are lightly browned; cool on
trays. Serve 1½ florentines
with 2 scoops of ice-cream.

serves 8
per serving 3.4g fat; 599kJ
(143 cal); 1.4g saturated fat;
0.7g fibre; 25.2g carbohydrate;
medium GI

pear oatmeal cake

PREPARATION TIME 15 MINUTES (PLUS STANDING TIME) **COOKING TIME** 1 HOUR

2 x 425g cans pear halves
    in syrup
1 cup (90g) rolled oats
½ cup (125g) low-fat
    dairy-free spread
½ teaspoon vanilla essence
¾ cup (150g) firmly packed
    brown sugar
2 eggs
¾ cup (110g) white
    self-raising flour
¾ cup (120g) wholemeal
    self-raising flour
½ teaspoon bicarbonate
    of soda
2 teaspoons ground ginger

1 Preheat oven to moderately hot. Grease and line sides of deep 23cm-square cake pan.
2 Drain pears over small saucepan. Heat syrup with oats, remove from heat; stand 20 minutes.
3 Meanwhile, using electric mixer, beat spread, vanilla and sugar in small bowl until combined. Beat in eggs, one at a time, until combined.
4 Add oat mixture and combined sifted remaining ingredients; stir until well combined. Pour mixture into prepared pan; place pears on top, cut-side down.
5 Bake, uncovered, in moderately hot oven about 55 minutes. Serve warm.

serves 16
per serving 4.5g fat; 720kJ (170 cal); 0.8g saturated fat; 2.6g fibre; 30g carbohydrate; medium GI

pink grapefruit granita with hazelnut wafers

PREPARATION TIME 20 MINUTES (PLUS FREEZING TIME) **COOKING TIME** 10 MINUTES

You will need two large pink grapefruit for this recipe.

1 cup (250ml) water
1 cup (220g) sugar
1 cup (250ml) fresh pink grapefruit juice
¼ cup (60ml) lemon juice
2 egg whites
HAZELNUT WAFERS
1 egg white
¼ cup (55g) caster sugar
2 tablespoons hazelnut meal
20g low-fat dairy-free spread, melted

1 Stir the water and sugar in small saucepan over heat, without boiling, until sugar dissolves. Bring to a boil; boil 5 minutes without stirring. Remove from heat; stir in juices, cool.

2 Using electric mixer, beat egg whites in small bowl until soft peaks form. Fold grapefruit syrup into egg white mixture; pour into 10cm x 24cm loaf pan. Cover; freeze 3 hours or overnight.

3 Blend or process granita until pale and creamy. Return to loaf pan, cover; freeze 3 hours or overnight. Serve granita with hazelnut wafers.
hazelnut wafers Preheat oven to moderate. Grease two oven trays; line each with baking paper. Using electric mixer, beat egg white in small bowl until soft peaks form; gradually add sugar, beating until sugar dissolves between additions. Add hazelnut meal and spread; stir until combined. Trace 16 x 7cm circles, 2cm apart, on lined trays. Spread a teaspoon of mixture in each circle. Bake in moderate oven about 5 minutes or until lightly browned. Cool wafers on trays before carefully peeling away paper.

serves 8
per serving 2.3g fat; 713kJ (170 cal); 0.2g saturated fat; 0.2g fibre; 36.7g carbohydrate; medium GI

pears poached in cranberry syrup

PREPARATION TIME 5 MINUTES (PLUS STANDING TIME) **COOKING TIME** 45 MINUTES

3 cups (750ml) cranberry juice
⅔ cup (160ml) dry white wine
2 cardamom pods, bruised
½ vanilla bean,
   halved lengthways
4 medium beurre bosc
   pears (920g)

1 Combine juice, wine,
  cardamom and vanilla bean
  in large saucepan.
2 Add peeled pears to pan; bring
  to a boil. Reduce heat; simmer,
  covered, about 25 minutes or
  until tender. Cool pears in syrup.
3 Remove pears from syrup;
  strain syrup into medium
  heatproof bowl. Return 2 cups
  of the strained syrup to same
  pan (discard remaining syrup);
  bring to a boil. Boil, uncovered,
  about 15 minutes or until syrup
  is reduced by half. Serve pears,
  hot or cold, with syrup.

serves 4
per serving 0.2g fat; 1178kJ
(281 cal); 0g saturated fat;
3.5g fibre; 26.5g carbohydrate;
low GI

tip Pears can be poached
a day ahead; reduce the syrup
just before serving.

If beurre bosc pears are
unavailable, use packham
or williams pears

apricot strudel

PREPARATION TIME 20 MINUTES **COOKING TIME** 20 MINUTES

825g can apricot slices in
   natural syrup, drained
2 tablespoons brown sugar
1 teaspoon ground cinnamon
¾ cup (120g) sultanas
¼ cup (35g) roasted hazelnuts,
   chopped finely
6 sheets fillo pastry
1 tablespoon no-fat milk
1 tablespoon icing
   sugar mixture

1 Preheat oven to moderately hot.
   Grease oven tray.
2 Combine apricots, sugar,
   cinnamon, sultanas and nuts
   in medium bowl.
3 Stack fillo sheets, brushing each
   lightly with milk as you layer.
   Spread apricot filling over fillo,
   leaving 5cm space at edge of
   both short sides and 2cm at
   edge of one long side. Fold short
   sides over; starting from filled
   long-side edge, roll strudel to
   enclose filling. Place, seam-side
   down, on prepared tray.
4 Brush strudel with remaining
   milk. Bake, uncovered, in
   moderately hot oven about
   25 minutes or until lightly
   browned. Dust strudel with icing
   sugar before serving, warm or
   cold, with ice-cream, if desired.

serves 6
per serving 2.6g fat; 585kJ
(143 cal); 0.2g saturated fat;
2g fibre; 20.6g carbohydrate;
medium GI

apple bread pudding

PREPARATION TIME 20 MINUTES
COOKING TIME 1 HOUR 10 MINUTES (PLUS STANDING TIME)

2 medium apples (300g)
2 tablespoons brown sugar
1 tablespoon water
2½ cups (625ml) no-fat milk
1 vanilla bean, halved lengthways
4 slices thick fruit bread
3 eggs
½ teaspoon ground cinnamon
¼ teaspoon ground nutmeg

1 Peel, core and quarter apples; cut each quarter into 3mm slices.
   Dissolve brown sugar in the water in medium frying pan over low heat,
   add apples; simmer, uncovered, about 5 minutes or until tender,
   stirring occasionally.
2 Preheat oven to moderately slow. Grease deep 1.5-litre (6 cup)
   ovenproof dish.
3 Combine milk and vanilla bean in medium saucepan; bring to a boil.
   Remove from heat; stand, covered, 5 minutes. Discard vanilla bean.
4 Meanwhile, cut bread slices into quarters. Arrange bread and apple
   in alternate layers in prepared dish.
5 Whisk eggs, cinnamon and nutmeg in medium bowl. Gradually whisk
   hot milk mixture into egg mixture. Pour egg mixture carefully over bread
   and apple. Place dish in large baking dish; add enough boiling water
   to baking dish to come halfway up side of pudding dish.
6 Bake, uncovered, in moderately slow oven about 1 hour or until set.
   Serve with low-fat ice-cream or cream, if desired.

serves 6
per serving 3.6g fat; 698kJ (167 cal); 1.1g saturated fat;
1.7g fibre; 25.5g carbohydrate; low GI

strawberry and rhubarb muffins

PREPARATION TIME 15 MINUTES **COOKING TIME** 20 MINUTES

You need about 4 large trimmed rhubarb stems for this recipe.

125g strawberries, sliced thinly
3 cups (450g) wholemeal
   self-raising flour
½ cup (100g) firmly packed
   brown sugar
1 teaspoon ground cinnamon
1 teaspoon vanilla essence
60g low-fat dairy-free
   spread, melted
¾ cup (180ml) no-fat soy milk
2 eggs, beaten lightly
2 cups (250g) finely
   chopped rhubarb
¼ cup (60g) apple sauce

1 Preheat oven to moderately hot.
   Grease 12-hole (⅓ cup/80ml)
   muffin pan. Reserve 12 slices
   of strawberry.
2 Combine flour, sugar and
   cinnamon in large bowl. Add
   essence, spread, milk and eggs;
   mix to combine then gently stir
   in remaining strawberries,
   rhubarb and apple sauce.
3 Divide mixture among holes of
   prepared pan; top each with a
   reserved strawberry slice. Bake
   in moderately hot oven about
   20 minutes. Serve warm or
   at room temperature.

makes 12
per muffin 4.3g fat; 844kJ
(202 cal); 0.8g saturated fat;
5.2g fibre; 34.2g carbohydrate;
medium GI

berry mousse

2 teaspoons gelatine
2 tablespoons water
2 egg whites
⅓ cup (75g) caster sugar
2 x 200g cartons low-fat
  berry-flavoured yogurt
150g fresh mixed berries

1 Sprinkle gelatine over the water
   In small heatproof jug; place jug
   in small pan of simmering water,
   stir until gelatine dissolves, cool.
2 Meanwhile, using electric
   mIxer, beat egg whites in small
   bowl until soft peaks form.
   Gradually add sugar, beating
   until sugar dissolves.
3 Place yogurt in medium bowl;
   stir in gelatine mixture, fold in
   egg white mixture. Spoon
   mousse mixture into serving
   bowl, cover; refrigerate about
   2 hours or until set. Top mousse
   with berries to serve.

serves 4
per serving 0.2g fat; 708kJ
(169 cal); 0.1g saturated fat;
0.9g fibre; 32.8g carbohydrate;
low GI

plum and cinnamon cake

PREPARATION TIME 15 MINUTES **COOKING TIME** 35 MINUTES

½ cup (125g) low-fat dairy-free spread
1 teaspoon vanilla essence
½ cup (100g) firmly packed brown sugar
3 eggs, separated
½ cup (75g) white self-raising flour
½ cup (80g) wholemeal self-raising flour
1 teaspoon ground cinnamon
4 whole canned plums in syrup, drained, halved, seeded

tip You'll probably have to open an 810g can of whole plums in syrup to get the required amount for this recipe. You can serve the remaining plums alongside this cake, or you can freeze them (in the syrup) until you wish to use them for another recipe.

1 Preheat oven to moderate. Grease 20cm ring pan; line base and sides with baking paper.
2 Using electric mixer, beat spread, essence, sugar and egg yolks in small bowl until light and fluffy. Transfer mixture to medium bowl; stir in flours and cinnamon.
3 Using electric mixer, beat egg whites in small bowl until soft peaks form; gently fold whites into cake batter.
4 Spread batter into prepared pan; place plums on top, cut-side down. Bake, uncovered, in moderate oven about 30 minutes. Stand 10 minutes; turn onto wire rack, turn top-side up to cool. Serve dusted with icing sugar mixture, if desired.

serves 12
per serving 6.8g fat; 832kJ (198 cal); 2.5g saturated fat; 1.2g fibre; 18.6g carbohydrate; medium GI

Canned plums generally hold their shape well when used in baking, and they don't lose any of their sweet flavour

chocolate brownie

PREPARATION TIME 15 MINUTES **COOKING TIME** 25 MINUTES

2 eggs
⅓ cup (75g) firmly packed
　brown sugar
2 teaspoons instant
　coffee powder
2 tablespoons cocoa powder
1 tablespoon water
1 tablespoon olive oil
40g low-fat dairy-free
　spread, melted
¼ cup (40g) wholemeal
　self-raising flour
¼ cup (45g) dark chocolate
　Choc Bits
1 teaspoon cocoa
　powder, extra
2 teaspoons icing sugar mixture

1　Preheat oven to moderate. Grease
　and line deep 19cm-square pan.
2　Using electric mixer, beat eggs
　and sugar in small bowl until
　thick and creamy. Transfer to
　medium bowl.
3　Meanwhile, blend coffee and
　cocoa with the water and oil in
　small bowl until smooth. Stir in
　spread. Fold cocoa mixture
　into egg mixture; fold in flour
　and Choc Bits. Pour mixture
　into prepared pan.
4　Bake, uncovered, in moderate
　oven about 25 minutes or until
　brownie is firm to the touch.
　Stand 30 minutes; turn onto wire
　rack. Serve brownie dusted with
　sifted combined extra cocoa
　and icing sugar mixture, and
　low-fat ice-cream, if desired.

makes 16
per brownie 3.8g fat; 303kJ
(73 cal); 0.6g saturated fat;
0.2g fibre; 4.7g carbohydrate;
medium GI

wholemeal date loaf

PREPARATION TIME 20 MINUTES **COOKING TIME** 1 HOUR

1 cup (170g) seeded
  dates, halved
2 tablespoons boiling water
½ teaspoon bicarbonate
  of soda
60g low-fat dairy-free spread
2 teaspoons finely grated
  lemon rind
¾ cup (150g) firmly packed
  brown sugar
200g low-fat cottage cheese
2 eggs
2 cups (320g) wholemeal
  self-raising flour
2 tablespoons wheat germ

1 Preheat oven to moderately slow.
   Grease 14cm x 21cm loaf pan;
   line base and two long sides
   with baking paper, extending
   paper 5cm above edges of pan.
2 Combine dates, the water and
   bicarbonate of soda in small
   bowl, cover; stand 5 minutes.
3 Using electric mixer, beat spread,
   rind and sugar in small bowl until
   light and fluffy. Add cheese; beat
   until smooth. Add eggs, one at
   a time; beat until combined.
4 Stir in flour, wheat germ and date
   mixture; pour into prepared pan.
5 Bake, uncovered, in moderately
   slow oven about 1 hour. Stand
   10 minutes; turn onto wire
   rack to cool.

serves 14
per serving 3.2g fat; 779kJ
(186 cal); 0.5g saturated fat;
2.9g fibre; 23.7g carbohydrate;
high GI

chocolate ricotta tart

PREPARATION TIME 15 MINUTES (PLUS REFRIGERATION TIME) **COOKING TIME** 35 MINUTES

¼ cup (35g) white self-raising flour
¼ cup (40g) wholemeal self-raising flour
2 tablespoons caster sugar
2 teaspoons cocoa powder
30g low-fat dairy-free spread
2 teaspoons water
1 egg yolk
RICOTTA FILLING
150g low-fat ricotta
1 egg
1 egg yolk
¼ cup (70g) low-fat yogurt
¼ cup (55g) caster sugar
2 teaspoons white plain flour
2 tablespoons dark Choc Bits
2 teaspoons coffee-flavoured liqueur

1 Grease 18cm-round loose-based flan tin.

2 Process flours, sugar, sifted cocoa and spread until crumbly;
add the water and egg yolk, process until ingredients just cling
together. Knead dough gently on lightly floured surface until smooth,
cover; refrigerate 30 minutes.

3 Preheat oven to moderately hot.

4 Press dough into prepared tin; cover with baking paper large
enough to extend 5cm over edge, fill with dried beans or rice. Bake,
on oven tray, in moderately hot oven 10 minutes; remove beans and
paper. Bake further 5 minutes or until pastry is lightly browned; cool.

5 Reduce temperature to moderate. Pour ricotta filling into tin;
bake, uncovered, in moderate oven about 20 minutes. Cool;
refrigerate until firm.

ricotta filling Using electric mixer, beat ricotta, egg, egg yolk,
yogurt, sugar and flour in medium bowl until smooth. Stir in
Choc Bits and liqueur.

serves 8
per serving 6.5g fat; 706kJ (169 cal); 2.9g saturated fat;
1.2g fibre; 21g carbohydrate; medium GI

Choc Bits are great to use
when baking because they
hold their shape and add an
explosive chocolatey crunch

apricot upside-down cakes

PREPARATION TIME 20 MINUTES **COOKING TIME** 20 MINUTES

1 tablespoon brown sugar
12 canned apricot halves
  in syrup, drained
2 eggs
¾ cup (150g) firmly packed
  brown sugar, extra
¾ cup (90g) almond meal
1 teaspoon vanilla essence
⅓ cup (50g) wholemeal
  self-raising flour
½ cup (125ml) no-fat milk
¼ cup (80g) light apricot
  conserve, heated

1 Preheat oven to moderate.
  Grease 12-hole (⅓ cup/80ml)
  muffin pan.
2 Sprinkle sugar equally into holes
  of prepared pan; add 1 apricot
  half, cut-side down, to each hole.
3 Using electric mixer, beat eggs
  and extra sugar in medium
  bowl until light and fluffy. Stir in
  almond meal, essence, flour
  and milk. Divide mixture among
  holes of prepared pan.
4 Bake in moderate oven about
  20 minutes. Stand 5 minutes;
  turn onto wire rack, brush
  apricot conserve over hot
  cakes. Serve cakes warm
  or at room temperature.

makes 12 cakes
per cake 5.2g fat; 554kJ
(132 cal); 0.6g saturated fat;
1.4g fibre; 18.2g carbohydrate;
medium GI

tip You'll probably have to open
a 415g can of apricot halves to
get the required amount for this
recipe. Serve the remaining
apricot halves with the cakes.

· fig-topped cheesecake

PREPARATION TIME 25 MINUTES (PLUS REFRIGERATION TIME)

"Nice" biscuits make a perfect base for this yummy cheesecake.

11 plain sweet biscuits (135g)
2 teaspoons gelatine
2 tablespoons water
200g low-fat yogurt
250g light cream
   cheese, softened
¼ cup (90g) honey
1 teaspoon ground cardamom
2 fresh figs (120g), cut
   into wedges

1 Grease deep 19cm-square cake pan; line base and sides with baking paper, extending 5cm above two opposing sides of pan.
2 Place biscuits in prepared pan; trim to cover base in a single layer.
3 Sprinkle gelatine over the water in small heatproof jug; place jug in small pan of simmering water, stir until gelatine dissolves. Cool 5 minutes.
4 Using electric mixer, beat yogurt and cream cheese in small bowl until smooth. Stir in honey and cardamom then gelatine mixture; pour into prepared pan. Cover; refrigerate about 4 hours or until set. Serve cheesecake topped with fig.

serves 16
per serving 3.6g fat; 387kJ (92 cal); 1.3g saturated fat; 0.2g fibre; 6.6g carbohydrate; medium GI

moist orange cake

PREPARATION TIME 15 MINUTES **COOKING TIME** 20 MINUTES (PLUS STANDING TIME)

4 large oranges (1.2kg)
60g low-fat dairy-free spread
1 cup (220g) caster sugar
2 eggs
⅓ cup (40g) almond meal
1 cup (160g) wholemeal self-raising flour
2 tablespoons no-fat soy milk

1 Preheat oven to moderately slow. Grease and line shallow
   23cm-round cake pan.
2 Finely grate ½ teaspoon of rind from 1 orange; slice 1 tablespoon
   of thin strips of rind from same orange. Reserve rinds. Squeeze the
   peeled orange; reserve ⅔ cup (160ml) juice. Peel remaining 3 oranges;
   separate into segments. Reserve segments.
3 Using electric mixer, beat spread, ⅓ cup of the sugar and the finely
   grated rind in small bowl until pale and creamy. Add eggs; beat until
   combined. Add almond meal, flour, 1 tablespoon of the orange juice
   and milk; stir to combine. Spread batter into prepared pan. Bake,
   uncovered, in moderately slow oven about 20 minutes.
4 Meanwhile, combine remaining juice and remaining sugar in small
   saucepan over heat, without boiling, until sugar dissolves; bring to
   a boil. Add reserved rind strips, reduce heat; simmer, uncovered,
   about 3 minutes or until syrup thickens slightly.
5 Remove cake from oven. Stand 5 minutes; turn onto wire rack. Using
   skewer, pierce cake several times; brush with ¼ cup of the hot syrup.
   Serve cake sliced, with reserved orange segments and remaining syrup.

serves 12
per serving 5.3g fat; 755kJ (180 cal); 0.8g saturated fat;
2.5g fibre; 30.7g carbohydrate; medium GI

raspberry yogurt cake

PREPARATION TIME 30 MINUTES **COOKING TIME** 1 HOUR 5 MINUTES

½ cup (125g) low-fat dairy-free spread
¾ cup (165g) firmly packed brown sugar
2 eggs
1¼ cups (200g) wholemeal self-raising flour
½ cup (140g) low-fat yogurt
100g frozen raspberries
CREAM-CHEESE FROSTING
80g light cream cheese, softened
⅓ cup (55g) icing sugar mixture
1 teaspoon lemon juice

1 Preheat oven to moderate. Grease 14cm x 21cm loaf pan;
   line base and two long sides with baking paper, extending paper
   5cm above edges of pan.
2 Using electric mixer, beat spread and sugar in medium bowl until light
   and fluffy. Add eggs, one at a time, beating until just combined.
3 Transfer mixture to medium bowl; stir in flour, yogurt and raspberries.
   Spread mixture into prepared pan.
4 Bake, uncovered, in moderate oven about 1 hour 5 minutes. Stand
   10 minutes, turn onto wire rack; turn top-side up to cool. Place cake on
   serving plate; using spatula, spread cake top with cream-cheese frosting.
   cream-cheese frosting Whisk cheese, sugar and lemon juice
   in small bowl until smooth.

serves 12
per serving 6.5g fat; 777kJ (186 cal); 1.7g saturated fat;
2.3g fibre; 28g carbohydrate; medium GI

Raspberries are a great
addition to this delicious
cake with their delicate
flavour and tender texture

vanilla bean ice-cream with espresso sauce

PREPARATION TIME 10 MINUTES (PLUS FREEZING TIME) **COOKING TIME** 15 MINUTES (PLUS STANDING TIME)

1 vanilla bean
1 cup (250ml) light evaporated milk
⅓ cup (80ml) light cream
2 egg yolks
½ cup (110g) caster sugar
½ cup (125ml) boiling water
1 tablespoon ground espresso coffee beans

1 Split vanilla bean lengthways; scrape seeds into small saucepan.
   Add vanilla bean, evaporated milk and cream; bring to a boil. Remove
   pan from heat, cover; stand 20 minutes. Discard vanilla bean.
2 Meanwhile, using electric mixer, beat egg yolks and sugar in small
   bowl until thick and creamy; gradually stir in vanilla mixture.
3 Return mixture to same pan; cook, stirring, over low heat, about
   15 minutes or until mixture thickens slightly (do not allow to boil).
4 Strain ice-cream mixture into 20cm x 30cm lamington pan, cover
   surface with foil; cool to room temperature. Freeze until almost set.
5 Place ice-cream in large bowl; chop coarsely. Using electric mixer,
   beat ice-cream until smooth. Pour into 14cm x 21cm loaf pan, cover;
   freeze until ice-cream is firm.
6 Just before serving, combine the water and coffee in coffee plunger; stand
   2 minutes before plunging. Cool 5 minutes before serving over ice-cream.

serves 4
per serving 7g fat; 965kJ (231 cal); 3.7g saturated fat;
0g fibre; 35.6g carbohydrate; medium GI

yogurt and mango jelly

PREPARATION TIME 5 MINUTES (PLUS REFRIGERATION TIME)

You need about 2 passionfruit for this recipe.

85g packet mango jelly crystals
1 cup (250ml) boiling water
2 x 200g cartons low-fat
   five-fruits yogurt
1 medium mango (430g),
   chopped finely
1 medium banana (200g),
   sliced thinly
1 medium kiwi fruit (85g),
   halved, sliced thinly
2 tablespoons passionfruit pulp

1 Stir jelly crystals with the
   water in small heatproof bowl
   until dissolved; refrigerate
   about 20 minutes or until
   cold (do not allow to set).
2 Add yogurt and mango to jelly;
   stir to combine. Divide jelly
   mixture among six 1-cup (250ml)
   serving glasses. Cover; refrigerate
   about 2 hours or until set. Just
   before serving, top each jelly
   with equal amounts of banana,
   kiwi fruit and passionfruit.

serves 6
per serving 1g fat; 720kJ
(172 cal); 0.5g saturated fat;
2.6g fibre; 36.3g carbohydrate;
low GI
tip We used golden kiwi fruit
in this recipe.

glossary

all-bran low-fat, high-fibre breakfast cereal based on wheat bran.

almonds

blanched: skins removed.

flaked: paper-thin slices of almond.

meal: also known as finely ground almonds; powdered to a flour-like texture and used as a thickening agent or in baking.

slivered: lengthways-cut almond pieces.

apple cider a beverage made by pressing the juice from apples; sold in two varieties, fresh "sweet" cider and "hard" cider (after fermentation). Alcoholic content ranges widely.

baking powder a raising agent consisting mainly of two parts cream of tartar to one part bicarbonate of soda (baking soda). The acid and alkaline combination, when moistened and heated, gives off carbon dioxide which aerates and lightens the mixture during baking.

barley a nutritious grain used in soups and stews as well as in whisky- and beer-making. Pearl barley has had the husk discarded and been hulled and polished, much the same as rice.

barley flakes also known as rolled barley, and steamed and rolled barley; flattened grains produced by steaming the barley grain then rolling it into flakes. Used as a thickener in soups and stews; also used to make porridges and muesli, and toppings for crumbles.

beef

eye fillet: tenderloin; good for roasting and barbecuing.

mince: also known as ground beef.

rump steak: boneless tender cut, rib eye, sirloin and fillet steak are all suitable substitutes.

beetroot also known as red beets or just beets; firm, round root vegetable. Can be eaten raw, grated, in salads, boiled and sliced, or roasted and mashed like potatoes.

bicarbonate of soda also known as baking or carb soda.

biscuits also known as cookies.

nice: an uniced, plain sweet biscuit topped with a sprinkle of sugar; good for making the crust for cheesecakes.

sweet: any plain sweet biscuit (or cookie) can be used as long as they are neither filled nor iced.

black mustard seeds also known as brown mustard seeds; more pungent than the white (or yellow) seeds used in most prepared mustards.

bok choy also known as bak choy, pak choy, chinese white cabbage and chinese chard; has a mild mustard taste. Use both stems and leaves: stir-fried, braised, or raw in salads. Baby bok choy is smaller and more tender, and often cooked whole.

breadcrumbs

packaged: fine-textured, crunchy, purchased, white breadcrumbs.

stale: one- or two-day-old bread made into crumbs by grating, blending or processing.

broccolini a cross between broccoli and Chinese kale, broccolini is milder and sweeter than broccoli. Each long stem is topped by a loose floret that closely resembles broccoli. Broccolini is completely edible, from floret to stem. Substitute Chinese broccoli (gai lam) or broccoli if you are unable to find it.

barbecue sauce a spicy tomato-based sweet sauce used to marinate or baste, or as an accompaniment.

buckwheat a herb in the same plant family as rhubarb; not a cereal so is gluten free. Available as flour (used to make blini and soba), coarsely ground, or whole and hulled (groats). Kasha, roasted buckwheat groats, is cooked like rice and has a nutty toasty flavour.

burghul also known as bulghur wheat. Hulled steamed wheat kernels that, once dried, are crushed into various-sized grains; not the same as cracked wheat. Used in Middle-Eastern dishes such as kibbeh and tabbouleh.

buttermilk sold alongside fresh milk products in supermarkets; despite the implication of its name, is low in fat. Commercially made, by a method similar to yogurt. A good low-fat substitution for dairy products such as cream or sour cream; good in baking, sauces and salad dressings.

cannellini bean small, dried white bean similar in both appearance and flavour to other *Phaseolus vulgaris* varieties such as great northern, navy or haricot beans. Sometimes sold as butter beans.

capsicum also known as bell pepper or, simply, pepper. Native to Central and South America, they can be red, green, yellow, orange or purplish black. Seeds and membranes should be discarded before use.

cardamom native to India and used extensively in its cuisine; it can be purchased in pod, seed or ground form. Has a distinctive aromatic, sweetly rich flavour and is one of the world's most expensive spices.

celeriac also known as celery root or celery knob; a tuberous root vegetable with brown skin, white flesh and a celery-like flavour.

cheese

cheddar: the most widely eaten cheese in the world; a semi-hard cow-milk cheese originally made in England. We used a low-fat variety with a fat content of not more than 7g per 25g.

cream: commonly known as Philadelphia or Philly; a mild-flavoured fresh cheese made of cow milk. It is an acid curd cheese that needs a starter culture of bacteria. We used one with 21g fat per 100g.

mozzarella: this soft, spun-curd cheese originated in southern Italy where it is traditionally made from water buffalo milk. Cow-milk versions of this product, commonly known as pizza cheese, are now available. We used one with 17.5g fat per 100g.

ricotta: a low-fat, fresh unripened cheese with 3g fat per 100g.

chickpeas also called garbanzos, hummus or channa; an irregularly round, sandy-coloured legume used extensively in Mediterranean cooking.

chinese broccoli also known as gai lam; used more for its stems than coarse leaves.

chinese cabbage also known as Peking cabbage or wong bok.

choy sum also known as flowering bok choy or flowering white cabbage.

cooking-oil spray we used a cholesterol-free cooking spray made from canola oil.

cornflour also known as cornstarch; used as a thickening agent.

cornmeal ground dried corn (maize); available in different textures.

couscous a fine, grain-like cereal product, originally from North Africa; made from semolina.

curry paste

tikka masala: literally meaning blended spices; a masala can be whole spices, a paste or a powder, and can include herbs as well as spices and other seasonings. Traditional dishes are usually based on and named after particular masalas. The word tikka means a bite-sized piece of meat, poultry or fish, or sometimes a cutlet. So, a jar labelled tikka masala usually contains the manufacturer's choice of spices and oils, mixed together to make a paste.

eggplant also known as aubergine.

essences also known as extracts; generally the by-product of distillation of plants.

flour

buckwheat: although not a true cereal, flour is made from its seeds. Available from health food stores.

self-raising: wholemeal or plain flour combined with baking powder in the proportion of 1 cup flour to 2 teaspoons baking powder.

white plain: an all-purpose flour, made from wheat.

ginger also known as green or root ginger; the thick gnarled root of a tropical plant. Can be kept, peeled, covered with dry sherry in a jar and refrigerated, or frozen in an airtight container.

golden syrup by-product of refined sugarcane; pure maple syrup or honey can be substituted.

ham we used light ham with a fat content of 2.3g per 100g, about half that of regular ham.

kasha also known as roasted buckwheat groats; has a nutty, richly toasty flavour and can be served like polenta, couscous or rice with a meat casserole or roast.

kecap manis Indonesian sweet, thick soy sauce which has sugar and spices added.

kumara the Polynesian name of orange-fleshed sweet potato, often confused with yam.

lavash flat, unleavened bread, originally from the Mediterranean.

lemon grass a tall, clumping, lemon-smelling and -tasting, sharp-edged grass; the white lower part of each stem is chopped and used in Asian cooking or for tea.

lentils dried pulses often identified by and named after their colour (red, brown or yellow); also known as dhal.

light sour cream we used a low-fat sour cream having a fat content of 18.5g per 100g.

linguine long, narrow pasta often thought of as a flat spaghetti.

low-fat cream we used cream having a fat content of 18%.

low-fat dairy-free spread we used Diet Becel, a commercial product having a fat content of 2.4g per 5g of spread (47g of fat per 100g of spread).

low-fat mayonnaise we used cholesterol-free mayonnaise having less than 3g fat per 100g.

low-fat thickened cream we used cream having a fat content of 18%.

low-fat yogurt we used yogurt having a fat content of less than 0.2%.

maple syrup distilled sap of the maple tree. Maple-favoured syrup is made from cane sugar and artificial maple flavouring and is not a substitute for the real thing.

mesclun mixed baby salad leaves also sold as salad mix or gourmet salad mix; a mixture of assorted young lettuce and other green leaves.

mince meat also known as ground meat.

mushrooms

button: small, cultivated white mushrooms having a delicate, subtle flavour.

swiss brown: light- to dark-brown mushrooms with full-bodied flavour. Button or cup mushrooms can be substituted for swiss brown mushrooms.

no-fat milk we used milk with a fat content of 0.15% or lower.

noodles

fresh rice: thick, wide, almost white in colour; made from rice and vegetable oil. Must be covered with boiling water to remove starch and excess oil before using in soups and stir-fries.

hokkien: also known as stir-fry noodles; fresh wheat noodles resembling thick, yellow-brown spaghetti and needing no pre-cooking before use.

rice stick: a dried noodle, available flat and wide or very thin; made from rice flour and water.

rice vermicelli: also known as rice-flour noodles and rice-stick noodles; made from ground rice. Sold dried, are best either deep-fried, or soaked then stir-fried or used in soups.

onion

brown and white: are interchangeable. Their pungent flesh adds flavour to a vast range of dishes.

green: also known as scallion or (incorrectly) shallot; an immature onion picked before the bulb has formed, having a long, bright-green edible stalk.

red: also known as spanish, red spanish or bermuda onion; a sweet, large, purple-red onion that is particularly good eaten raw in salads.

paprika ground, dried, red capsicum (bell pepper), available sweet or hot.

parsley, flat-leaf also known as continental parsley or italian parsley.

passionfruit also known as granadilla; a small tropical fruit, native to Brazil, comprised of a tough dark-purple skin surrounding edible black sweet-sour seeds.

pecan nut native to the United States; buttery, golden-brown and rich. Good in savoury as well as sweet dishes; especially good in salads.

pepitas the dried seeds of a pumpkin.

pide also known as turkish bread, comes in long (about 45cm) flat loaves as well as individual rounds. This bread is made from wheat flour and sprinkled with sesame or black onion seeds.

pitta also spelled pita and known as lebanese bread, this wheat-flour pocket bread is sold in large, flat pieces that separate easily into two thin rounds. Also available in small thick pieces called pocket pitta.

polenta a flour-like cereal made of ground corn (maize); ground cornmeal. Also the name of the dish made from it.

raisins large, dark-brown, dried, sweet grapes.

rhubarb a vegetable related to sorrel; only the firm, reddish stems are eaten. It's normally sweetened and eaten as a dessert.

rice

arborio: small, round-grain rice well-suited to absorb a large amount of liquid; especially suitable for making risottos.

basmati: a white fragrant long-grain rice. It should be washed several times before cooking.

doongara: a recently released strain of long-grain rice, previously only produced in tropical climates. Has a lower GI (glycaemic index) rating than many other rice varieties; because it is more slowly absorbed into the blood stream, it helps provide sustained energy release. This rice can be overcooked for a few minutes beyond the recommended 12-minute cooking time and still result in fluffy, firm, separate grains.

jasmine: a fragrant long-grain rice; white rice can be substituted but will not taste the same.

rice paper sheets mostly from Vietnam (banh trang). Made from rice paste and stamped into rounds, with a woven pattern. Stores well at room temperature, although are quite brittle and break easily. Dipped momentarily in water, they become pliable wrappers for fried food and for wrapping around fresh (uncooked) vegetables.

risoni also known as risi; small rice-shaped pasta very similar to another small pasta, orzo.

rocket also known as arugula, rugula or rucola; a peppery-tasting green leaf which can be used similarly to baby spinach leaves. Can be used raw in salads or used in cooking. Baby rocket leaves are both smaller and less peppery.

rolled grains includes rice, barley, oats, rye and triticale; the whole grain has been steamed and flattened – not the quick-cook variety. Available from health food stores and supermarkets.

rosewater extract made from crushed rose petals; used for its aromatic quality in many desserts and sweets.

salted black beans also known as Chinese black beans, these are fermented and salted soy beans available in cans and jars. Used most often in Asian cooking; chop before, or mash during, cooking to release flavour.

sauces

fish: also called nam pla or nuoc nam; made from pulverised salted fermented fish, most often anchovies. Has a pungent smell and strong taste; use sparingly.

oyster: Asian in origin, this rich, brown sauce is made from oysters and their brine, cooked with salt and soy sauce, and thickened with starches.

soy: made from fermented soy beans. Many variations are available in most supermarkets; we used a mild Japanese variety.

sweet chilli: a relatively mild, Thai-type sauce made from red chillies, sugar, garlic and vinegar.

tomato pasta sauce, bottled: prepared sauce available from supermarkets; sometimes labelled sugo.

seed tapioca sometimes called sago because it comes from the sago palm pearl; tapioca is from the root of the cassava plant. Used in soups, desserts and often as a thickening agent; available from some supermarkets and most health-food stores.

semolina made from durum wheat; milled various-textured granules, all of these finer than flour. The main ingredient in good pastas, in some kinds of gnocchi and in many Middle-Eastern and Indian sweets.

silverbeet also known as seakale or swiss chard. A green-leafed vegetable with sturdy celery-like white stems. A member of the beet family, silverbeet can be used similarly to spinach.

skewers bamboo or metal skewers can be used. Rub oil onto metal skewers to stop meat sticking. Soak bamboo skewers in water for at least 1 hour before use to prevent splintering and scorching.

snow peas also called mange tout ("eat all"). Snow pea tendrils, the growing shoots of the plant, are sold by greengrocers.

Special K low-fat breakfast cereal based on rice and wheat; good source of calcium and iron.

spinach also known as English spinach and, incorrectly, silverbeet. The tender green leaves are good raw in salads or added to soups and stir-fries just before serving.

stock 1 cup (250ml) is equivalent to 1 cup (250ml) water plus 1 crumbled stock cube. It may be more convenient to use stock in tetra paks.

sugar we used coarse granulated table sugar, also known as crystal sugar, unless stated otherwise.

brown: an extremely soft, fine granulated sugar retaining molasses for its characteristic colour and flavour.

caster: also known as finely granulated table sugar.

icing sugar mixture: also known as confectioners' sugar or powdered sugar; granulated sugar crushed together with a small amount (about 3%) cornflour added.

sultanas small dried grapes, also known as golden raisins.

sumac a purple-red, astringent spice ground from berries growing on Mediterranean shrubs; adds a tart flavour to dips and dressings. Available from Middle-Eastern food stores.

sunflower seed kernels kernels from dried, husked sunflower seeds.

taco shells commercially prepared deep-fried corn tortillas folded over to create a container for various fillings.

tamarind paste made from the pods of a tree native to India that contain a sour-sweet pulp that is dried then reconstituted to make the dark, thick paste that adds a tangy astringent taste to curries. It can also be used in marinades and bastes for meats.

tofu also known as bean curd; an off-white, custard-like product made from the milk of crushed soy beans. Available fresh as soft or firm, and processed as fried or pressed dried sheets. Silken tofu refers to the method by which it is made — where it is strained through silk.

tortilla unleavened bread sold frozen, fresh or vacuum-packed; made from either wheat flour or corn (maize meal).

tomato

cherry: also known as Tiny Tim or Tom Thumb tomatoes; small and round.

egg: also called plum or Roma; these are smallish oval-shaped tomatoes much used in Italian cooking or salads.

triticale a nutritious hybrid of wheat (triticum) and rye (secale) which contains more protein and less gluten than wheat and has a nutty, sweet flavour. Available in whole grain, flour and flakes.

unprocessed bran made from the outer layer of a cereal – most often the husks of wheat, rice or oats.

vanilla bean dried, long, thin pod from a tropical orchid grown in Central and South America and Tahiti; the tiny black seeds inside the bean are used to impart a vanilla flavour in baking and desserts. Place whole bean in a container of sugar to make the vanilla sugar called for in recipes.

vietnamese mint not actually a mint at all, this narrow-leafed, pungent herb, also known as Cambodian mint and laksa leaf (daun laksa), is widely used in many Asian soups and salads.

vinegar

balsamic: authentic only from the province of Modena, Italy; made from a regional wine of white Trebbiano grapes specially processed then aged in antique wooden casks to give the exquisite pungent flavour.

red wine: based on fermented red wine.

white wine: made from fermented white wine.

wheat germ small creamy flakes milled from the embryo of the berry.

zucchini also known as courgette.

index

facts and figures

Wherever you live, you'll be able to use our recipes with the help of these easy-to-follow conversions. While these conversions are approximate only, the difference between an exact and the approximate conversion of various liquid and dry measures is but minimal, and will not affect your cooking results.

dry measures

metric	imperial
15g	½oz
30g	1oz
60g	2oz
90g	3oz
125g	4oz (¼lb)
155g	5oz
185g	6oz
220g	7oz
250g	8oz (½lb)
280g	9oz
315g	10oz
345g	11oz
375g	12oz (¾lb)
410g	13oz
440g	14oz
470g	15oz
500g	16oz (1lb)
750g	24oz (1½lb)
1kg	32oz (2lb)

liquid measures

metric	imperial
30ml	1 fluid oz
60ml	2 fluid oz
100ml	3 fluid oz
125ml	4 fluid oz
150ml	5 fluid oz (¼ pint/1 gill)
190ml	6 fluid oz
250ml	8 fluid oz
300ml	10 fluid oz (½ pint)
500ml	16 fluid oz
600ml	20 fluid oz (1 pint)
1000ml (1 litre)	1¾ pints

helpful measures

metric	imperial
3mm	⅛in
6mm	¼in
1cm	½in
2cm	¾in
2.5cm	1in
5cm	2in
6cm	2½in
8cm	3in
10cm	4in
13cm	5in
15cm	6in
18cm	7in
20cm	8in
23cm	9in
25cm	10in
28cm	11in
30cm	12in (1ft)

measuring equipment

The difference between one country's measuring cups and another's is, at most, within a 2 or 3 teaspoon variance. (For the record, one Australian metric measuring cup holds approximately 250ml.) The most accurate way of measuring dry ingredients is to weigh them. When measuring liquids, use a clear glass or plastic jug with metric markings. (For the record, one Australian metric tablespoon holds 20ml; one Australian metric teaspoon holds 5ml.)

Note: NZ, Canada, US and UK use 15ml tablespoons. All cup and spoon measurements are level.

We use large eggs with an average weight of 60g.

how to measure

When using graduated metric measuring cups, shake dry ingredients loosely into the appropriate cup. Do not tap the cup on a bench or tightly pack the ingredients unless directed to do so. Level top of measuring cups and measuring spoons with a knife. When measuring liquids, place a clear glass or plastic jug with metric markings on a flat surface to check accuracy at eye level.

oven temperatures

These oven temperatures are only a guide. Always check the manufacturer's manual.

	°C (Celsius)	°F (Fahrenheit)	Gas Mark
Very slow	120	250	1
Slow	150	300	2
Moderately slow	160	325	3
Moderate	180 – 190	350 – 375	4
Moderately hot	200 – 210	400 – 425	5
Hot	220 – 230	450 – 475	6
Very hot	240 – 250	500 – 525	7

Looking after **your interest...**

Keep your ACP cookbooks clean, tidy and within easy reach with slipcovers designed to hold up to 12 books. Plus you can follow our recipes perfectly with a set of accurate measuring cups and spoons, as used by *The Australian Women's Weekly* Test Kitchen.

To order

Mail or fax Photocopy and complete the coupon below and post to ACP Books Reader Offer, ACP Publishing, GPO Box 4967, Sydney NSW 2001, or fax to (02) 9267 4967.

Phone Have your credit card details ready, then phone 136 116 (Mon-Fri, 8.00am-6.00pm; Sat, 8.00am-6.00pm).

Price

Book Holder

Australia: $13.10 (incl. GST).
Elsewhere: $A21.95.

Metric Measuring Set

Australia: $6.50 (incl. GST).
New Zealand: $A8.00.
Elsewhere: $A9.95.

Prices include postage and handling. This offer is available in all countries.

Payment

Australian residents

We accept the credit cards listed on the coupon, money orders and cheques.

Overseas residents

We accept the credit cards listed on the coupon, drafts in $A drawn on an Australian bank, and also British, New Zealand and U.S. cheques in the currency of the country of issue. Credit card charges are at the exchange rate current at the time of payment.

Test Kitchen Staff
Food director *Pamela Clark*
Food editor *Karen Hammial*
Assistant food editor *Amira Ibram*
Test kitchen manager *Kimberley Coverdale*
Senior home economist *Kellie Ann*
Home economists *Sammie Coryton,*
Kelly Cruickshanks, Cathie Lonnie,
Naomi Scesny, Jeanette Seamons,
Alison Webb, Danielle West
Editorial coordinator *Laura O'Brien*

ACP Books Staff
Editorial director *Susan Tomnay*
Creative director *Hieu Chi Nguyen*
Senior editor *Julie Collard*
Designer *Mary Keep*
Studio manager *Caryl Wiggins*
Editorial/sales coordinator *Caroline Lowry*
Editorial assistant *Karen Lai*
Publishing manager (sales) *Brian Cearnes*
Publishing manager (rights & new projects)
Jane Hazell
Brand manager *Donna Gianniotis*
Pre-press *Harry Palmer*
Production manager *Carol Currie*
Business manager *Seymour Cohen*
Assistant business analyst *Martin Howes*
Chief executive officer *John Alexander*
Group publisher *Pat Ingram*
Publisher *Sue Wannan*

Produced by ACP Books, Sydney.
Printed by Dai Nippon Printing in Korea.
Published by ACP Publishing Pty Limited,
54 Park St, Sydney; GPO Box 4088,
Sydney, NSW 2001.
Ph: (02) 9282 8618 Fax: (02) 9267 9438.
acpbooks@acp.com.au
www.acpbooks.com.au
To order books, phone 136 116.
Send recipe enquiries to:
recipeenquiries@acp.com.au
AUSTRALIA: Distributed by Network Services,
GPO Box 4088, Sydney, NSW 2001.
Ph: (02) 9282 8777 Fax: (02) 9264 3278.
UNITED KINGDOM: Distributed by Australian
Consolidated Press (UK), Moulton Park
Business Centre, Red House Rd,
Moulton Park, Northampton, NN3 6AQ.
Ph: (01604) 497 531 Fax: (01604) 497 533
acpukltd@aol.com
CANADA: Distributed by Whitecap Books Ltd,
351 Lynn Ave, North Vancouver, BC, V7J 2C4.
Ph: (604) 980 9852 Fax: (604) 980 8197
customerservice@whitecap.ca
www.whitecap.ca
NEW ZEALAND: Distributed by Netlink
Distribution Company, ACP Media Centre,
Cnr Fanshawe and Beaumont Streets,
Westhaven, Auckland.
PO Box 47906, Ponsonby, Auckland, NZ.
Ph: (09) 366 9966 ask@ndcnz.co.nz

Clark, Pamela.
The Australian Women's Weekly
Low-fat Food for Life.

Includes index.
ISBN 1 86396 292 1

1. Low-fat diet – recipes. I. Title.
II. Title: Low-fat Food for Life.
III. Title: Australian Women's Weekly.

641.5638

© ACP Publishing Pty Limited 2003
ABN 18 053 273 546

This publication is copyright. No part of it may be reproduced or transmitted in any form without the written permission of the publishers.
First published 2003. Reprinted 2004.
The publishers would like to thank the following for props used in photography:
Empire Homewares, Paddington, NSW;
Home Excellence, Drummoyne, NSW;
Mud Australia, Marrickville, NSW; and
Ventura Design, Lilyfield, NSW.

Photocopy and complete coupon below

- ☐ **Book Holder**
- ☐ **Metric Measuring Set**
  Please indicate number(s) required.

Mr/Mrs/Ms _____

Address _____

_____

Postcode _____ Country _____

Ph: Business hours ( ) _____

I enclose my cheque/money order for $ _____ payable to ACP Publishing.

OR: please charge my

- ☐ Bankcard ☐ Visa ☐ Mastercard
- ☐ Diners Club ☐ American Express

Card number

Card number

Expiry date ____ /____

Cardholder's signature _____

Please allow up to 30 days delivery within Australia.
Allow up to 6 weeks for overseas deliveries.
Both offers expire 31/12/04. HLLFFFL04